WHY AM I STILL SINGLE
For Women

The Truth I Wish My Mum Told Me
About Men

IEVA KAMBAROVAITE

WOW Book Publishing™

Dedication

I wrote this book so that you can LOVE. I know love is available for you.

I wrote this book so that you can LOVE yourself. The LOVE that can't be seen. It can only be felt.

I wrote this book so that you can understand you're enough and worthy to have everything you want in life.

Embrace your inner Goddess, the warrior of light, the woman that dances with wolves.

I wrote this book as a reminder for myself that I am enough, and I deserve LOVE.

Contents

Reviews of
Why Am I Still Single

I work with women. This book will be life-changing for so many of my clients. Ieva perfectly demonstrates the battle that so many of us are fighting trying to build empires while staying loving and in tune with our feminine power. Ieva makes you believe that you can have it all.

—Elmire Chicot, Author of *Libère Ton Pouvoir Féminin*. Coach for women entrepreneurs and Energy alchemist in Feminine power, LesDivinementBelles.com

My mission is to help as many people as I can to find the dating life they have always dreamed about. I wish all my clients would read this book to understand it's the inner work they must focus on if they want to be in a loving relationship with someone else.

—T. Anthony, Dating Coach, OnlineDatingSuperPowers.com

I had so much fun reading Ieva's first book for men *How To Get Laid Now*. I thought it was such a clever read and I am so happy to see she's got something for us ladies as well. *Why Am I Still Single For Women* is not just a regular book telling you how to get a man. It's a book that shows how to heal yourself and how to open up and invite the love you really deserve.

—Erikaa Briones, Sexual Confidence Coach,
founder of SexySoulCollective, ErikaBriones.com

I love that Ieva talks about communication and its importance in a relationship. I can see how so many of my clients would benefit from this book simply by learning how to express themselves more openly, which is also one of the key components to having great sex.

—Rebecca Mattas, Clinical Sexologist,
RebeccaMattas.com

I am still on my own personal journey trying to figure out what LOVE is all about. I really enjoyed Ieva's perspective, her honesty sharing her own experiences and had quite a few AHA moments. Now I know I can. I'd definitely recommend it to my girlfriends and my clients.

—Jasmina Legros, Author of *Strict Minimum*,
Founder and Chemical Engineer of the luxury
cosmetic brand Just What You Need, grouperys.fr

I work with female entrepreneurs who are focusing all their time and energy on their business, but they have neglected themselves and their relationships. I love that Ieva openly shares her own struggles on this journey and provides a number of ways one can start healing and having a better quality of life.

—Gia Gintaute Vitkute, Life Coach, GiaVitkute.com

The first time I met Ieva she took pictures of me. I was so surprised. It felt she could really see me. In this book it feels that she can really see and understand us ladies and our struggles when it comes to juggling a demanding career, self-love and great relationships. A must read even if you're not single.

—Shanaya Dawn Parr, artist, faery queen and creator, ShanayaDawnParr.com

If only this book was here a decade ago. It would have saved me so much headache and heartache. I love that Ieva shares her own personal journey, which makes me feel much better about myself. The body image issues, hours waiting for that text, going on another bad date or jumping to the next base way too soon. It doesn't matter what your struggle is, you'll find something for yourself.

—Selina Moestl, Author of the upcoming book *Never Forget to Sparkle—A Guide of How to Reach Your Personal Stars*, entrepreneur, RevitaliseYourLife.eu

I always thought that women didn't have to go through so much to find the right partner. Now I know we're not that different when it comes to chasing unavailable people, struggling to love and accept ourselves, going through a heartbreak or putting everyone else's needs before our own. I really appreciate that Ieva encourages women to go out and approach men. My single friends will be extremely grateful for this book.

—Moh Rahman: Moh Rahman, Transformational
Coach, EnergyFlowGenerator.com

About the Author

Ieva Kambarovaite is the award-winning author, speaker, relationship and dating coach. After her controversial debut *How to Get Laid Now: The Modern Man's Strategy to Approaching Women Like the Boss*, Ieva is finally showing women how to get out of their dating rut. She helps men and women, professionals and business owners, from all over the world to find love in all areas of their lives. You are most likely to run into Ieva if you are hanging out in one of the coffee shops in Nottingham, UK, where she currently lives when she is not feeding her never-ending wanderlust exploring foreign lands. Visit her at WhyAmIStillSingleBook.com

Foreword

This book will show you how to find love.

Why Am I Still Single is not your typical dating book. It is an entertaining and insightful guide showing a smart, driven and ambitious woman how to stop attracting the wrong men, how to heal herself, where to find love and your tribe, how to get clear about what you really want in life, how to love your body, how to get the date that makes you feel excited, how to look after yourself so you don't get burned out.

After reading this book, you will finally understand what is stopping you from meeting that special someone and finding love in your life. The answer is very simple and by implementing several steps presented in this book, you will see the most positive and exciting changes in all areas of your life.

This book can get you from a woman who thinks of 99 reasons why he has not texted you back, to someone who is seeing a man that cannot wait to call you.

Ieva shares her own personal journey on how she went from someone who was waiting for those blue ticks on WhatsApp to appear, to a woman that knows how to love herself, how to put herself first and how to build a life that does not just revolve around finding a partner.

Do you know how to communicate with him, so he understands you? Do you know why you feel lonely and broken? Do you know what you really want in your partner? Do you know your love language? Do you know why you keep attracting the wrong guys?

Learn the answers to these questions in *Why Am I Still Single*.

See instant results by making the most of the book. Don't just read it but take action from day one.

Ieva has put so much love into this book. It can heal your wounds and open the doors to a life full of love.

—Loral Langemeier
New York Times Bestselling Author
The Millionaire Maker
LiveOutLoud.com

Loral Langemeier: The Millionaire Maker, sought-after speaker, bestselling author, CEO and founder of *Integrated Wealth Systems*—a global platform dedicated to changing the conversation about the money and empowering people around the world to become millionaires. Loral was also one of the expert teachers featured in *The Secret*.

Acknowledgments

I would like to express my love and gratitude to the following people:

My sisters, Inara and Greta, for always supporting me and for not telling me I am crazy when I come up with another big thing.

Shraddha Chauhan for being my love and for all the beautiful vibes you send my way. I can feel them even if you are miles away.

My *Priority* bitches, Amanda, Tracey, Abi. You have no idea how much you have helped me. I felt loved and good enough.

Vishal Morjaria for being a great friend and for challenging me to get all the content for this book in 24 hours. I did it.

Loral Langemeier, Lisa Nichols, Dr Joe Dispenza, Marisa Peer, Les Brown, Leo Gura, Tom Bilyeu, Alain de Botton, John Gray, Jessica O'Reilly, Esther Perel, Adina Rivers, Lewis Howes, Mel Robbins, Marie Forleo, Brene Brown, Elizabeth Gilbert, Mathew Hussey, Sunny Lenarduzzi, for their knowledge, work, courage, and their commitment to their vision that is inspiring and life-transforming.

Finally, I would like to send my love to my future husband that I haven't met yet.

Baby, wait till you meet me. I am God's gift. A Goddess that knows what to do when a bird shits on her.

Why You Should Read This Book

I know you'd rather eat nothing but kale for the next two weeks than go on another bad date. I know you're focusing on building your empire or getting the promotion that's going to allow you to pay for that cute bag you don't need, but that you want. Being in a relationship is not even one of your biggest priorities.

You might even think that *The Notebook* is one of the cringiest films on this planet, but deep down you wish Ryan Gosling would come and smother you with all his love. Yes, I know. He's taken. For now (hahaha evil laugh).

You are smart and sophisticated, intelligent and independent. You are on your way to having it all, but for some reason you still get stuck in that mysterious game which involves checking your phone every 5 minutes to see if he's read your message. Thinking of 99 reasons he's not responding to you by ignoring the most obvious one. He's simply unavailable. In all imaginable ways.

Then you meet the nice guy who loves everything about you, even your cellulite. He wants to kiss you despite your terrible morning breath, but something just doesn't feel

Why Am I Still Single *For Women*

right. Is it you? Is it him? You start thinking the happily ever after is just not for you.

I have done all of those. Well, apart from the kale diet. I like kale, but not for two weeks straight. Chocolate is a whole different topic, but I still love you if you don't like chocolate. Weird though. Why? Why don't you like chocolate?

This book is for you, dear Goddess.

You're a fierce warrior of light, a woman that dances with wolves, the beautiful soul that was hurt too many times, but who still believes in LOVE.

Fifty Shades of Grey is like a
grownup Disney story with
a modern prince riding a
660-horsepower toy and rescuing
a beautiful girl from her misery.

—Ieva K.

CHAPTER I

Why You'll Marry the Wrong Person

1. Your Unhealthy Dating Pattern

Handsome, tall, dark. Unavailable.

Handsome, tall, dark. Unavailable.

Handsome, tall, dark. Unavailable.

Hi. My name is Ieva. I am a 31-year-old awesome young lady, a recovering unavailable man hunter. I am attracted to tall, dark handsome and unavailable. Still fighting my never-ending urge to go after the tall, dark, handsome and unavailable. At least now I know. It took me almost a decade to understand.

You might be someone who can't relate to this, because you're all about that blond, fair and short. But hear me out, sister. Let me take you on an unforgettable journey. It's safe in here. It's just You and me. I'm feeling rather emotional already. I don't have that many soul sisters that I can openly speak about the talk, dark, handsome and unavailable.

Have you ever wanted something you can't have? I remember being at the street market in Bangkok. Yes, I'm showing off how well travelled I am. I saw a pair of beautiful shoes and I wanted to take a picture. Then I saw a sign next to them saying 'Take a picture of me'. The second I saw it my desire to capture it disappeared. I just stood there observing my thoughts and thinking what a messed-up creature I was.

> *A disclaimer*: I am practicing kindness towards myself. I shall only speak to myself with words full of kindness. Please, join me. I have a feeling you could do with some of that goodness. Repeat after me: I'm a peaceful being full of love. I'm a peaceful being full of love. No giggles, please.

These shoes basically sum up my dating life for the last decade or so. I desire something I can't have. When it's too available I lose my interest. If he's all over me I like it at the very beginning, but then I get confused, because I don't know how to deal with someone who doesn't ignore my texts, doesn't cancel on me and thinks I am amazing just the way I am. Can you relate? If there is nothing messed up about him, if there's nothing I can fix about him, how can I contribute to this relationship?

Then I go back to what I know the best. I go back to tall, dark, handsome and unavailable. Someone who is not responding to my messages, someone who never calls me and only sees me when he wants to. Someone who keeps me as his biggest secret and tells me to hide in the car when I'm with him on his street, so no one can see me. Someone that tells me I'm the only woman in his life, but later I find out he's got a wife and two children.

And you know what the funniest part is? I'm not even exaggerating.

Now I am going to tell you a story about a young lady called Ieva and an unavailable man she was seeing. First, I thought I would pretend it is not about me. Really going out of my comfort zone here. But I feel slightly safer talking about it in the third person. The denial and the insecurity in me kick in. Repeat after me: I'm a peaceful being full of love.

Ieva and Mr Unavailable met at the coffee shop. She couldn't take her eyes off him. He was tall, dark and handsome. But it was more than that. It's the way he carried himself. She saw his piercing eyes and a lady next to him. The fact that he was with a lady made him even more attractive.

The time went by and they kept bumping into each other at the same coffee shop. He was kind of hanging around like a cat. Ieva loves cats, because they are independent and unavailable. Ieva and Mr Unavailable started talking and next thing you know he was picking her up from work, he was waiting by her door at 7AM just to say 'good morning'. #Romance.

They didn't exchange their phone numbers for the first two weeks. He just didn't ask her number. He would turn up unexpectedly and she loved all the excitement, suspense and the unknown.

Ieva and Mr Unavailable had a thing going on that went on for over a year. He would come and see her when he was available. He would make her wait for 4 hours. He'd not respond to her messages for 48 hours saying he had a family emergency or that he was unwell. He would come to her house and go to another room to take a phone call.

He would ask her not to speak to anyone or not to tell anyone about their relationship, because it was too special to be shared. Mr Unavailable introduced her to his friends, but he would never take her out. She still liked him, because he was tall, dark, handsome and unavailable.

Then Ieva found out that Mr Unavailable was indeed unavailable. The lady that Ieva saw him with at the coffee shop that day, the one he said he had nothing to do with anymore, was his Mrs, someone he's been living with for 6 years and continued to do so while seeing Ieva.

The most important thing about this story is that Ieva kind of knew from the very beginning that he was unavailable. She just chose to ignore it.

Now that you know Ieva's story I hope you will be able to look at your relationships and see if there's a pattern going on. You might not be able to relate to any of this. Please, continue reading. I am sure you'll find something for yourself even if you don't go after the tall, dark, handsome and unavailable.

2. Daddy's Girl

I have a confession to make. I am a self-development junkie. I love all things that tell me how my mind works, why I do what I do, where it stems from. I remember when I was still at school I would get back home and do personality tests I could find in magazines. Can you relate? Now it's all about YouTube.

One afternoon after hours just scrolling through YouTube and having one of those days where I'm not just binge watching 'what's in my bag', Kardashian success stories, makeup tutorials, even though I don't really wear much makeup, but I was looking for some answers.

I came across this very interesting video by Alain de Botton, philosopher and author, titled *Why You Will Marry The Wrong Person*.

"Anyone we might marry could, of course, be a little bit wrong for us. We don't expect bliss every day. We know that perfection is not on the cards. Nevertheless, there are couples who display such deep-seated incompatibility, such heightened rage and disappointment, that we have to conclude that something else is at play beyond the normal scratchiness: they appear to have married the wrong person . . ."[1]

As I was watching the video I had my 'A-Ha' moment. Alain de Botton had an answer to something I had been trying to figure out for the last decade. And it was not that I should have never even dated before getting to know myself first and my needs or that I could not make up my mind

1   Allan de Botton, *Why You Will Marry the Wrong Person*, The School of Life, 2014, https://www.youtube.com/watch?v=zuKV2DI9-Jg

who I would like to spend the rest of my life with or that my ex-boyfriends wouldn't make great fathers or stay loyal and sit next to my bed if I was suddenly dying from cancer. He gave me an answer to why I am attracted to unavailable men.

Did you grow up in a family were your parents were abusive, controlling, used to humiliate you? Do you feel that suffering is part of your childhood? Were your parents the most loving and lovely to you, but extremely abusive towards each other? And as much as they were trying to hide that from you and pretend everything was fine you could still see and feel what was happening.

What Alain de Botton says is that we are attracted to what is familiar to us, whether it's good or bad for us. That's when I realized that as much as it is painful for me to admit I am Daddy's girl.

I grew up with a dad that was abusive towards my mother in all possible ways. He never did anything to me or my sisters, but he was nasty towards my mum. When I was growing up I would always tell myself that I would never let anyone treat me this way.

However, an interesting thing is that even if you understand that a certain behaviour is wrong and is hurting you and you see that as a painful experience, and even if you consciously think that you will never ever let anyone treat you that way, unconsciously this is a full bouquet of qualities you are attracted to. It is something you are so used to.

You meet someone and at the very beginning it might be all roses, but very soon you feel that this person is neglecting you, is unavailable, makes you feel bad about yourself and makes you feel like you are not enough. However, the funniest thing is that you think that this is love, because when you were growing up this is what you experienced. It feels familiar. Even if you do all you can to go after someone who's loving and caring, you feel that something is missing. You are not used to it, because subconsciously you want the familiarity. You want pain.

If you can relate to any of that I have good news for you. You can heal yourself. I say that because I have spent years looking for answers and I have something very special for you that you can start doing today. Find out more by continuing to read this book. I am excited for you, dear Goddess.

3. Heal Yourself

I went on a retreat in Sicily. It was an amazing 7-day lifestyle and business retreat during which I was learning how to monetize and package my products, how to free myself from the blocks that are stopping me from making the most of my talents and gifts doing what I love the most. If you have never attended a retreat I would highly recommend you do it. It's an amazing experience. I might do my own retreat for a fierce lady like you.

During one of the first days of the retreat I was handed a questionnaire where I was asked a number of questions. There were examples of behaviours, qualities, habits, views towards certain aspects of life. I had to attribute them to either my mother or my father.

It was an eye-opening experience and I learned a lot about myself and how I view the world and the parts of me that I really want to focus on in order to heal myself and to have a life full of love and abundance. The life where I'm the

Queen, the fierce warrior of light, the Goddess, the woman that dances with wolves.

If you are on a journey where you would like to see a change in yourself and you are willing to work towards it, the first thing you can do is have a clear understanding of what is stopping you. Once you know that you can start the healing process.

What have I learned about myself? The main thing I have realized was that all the qualities that are stopping me in life, my lack of confidence and the low self-esteem, my habit of putting myself second, my lack of determination and my lack of assertiveness all come from my lovely mother.

However, when it comes to such qualities as being laid back, extremely confident, money-driven, focused, able to attract what you want, being extremely charismatic, these are the qualities I really admire in others, but I don't feel I am someone who possesses them. These are all the qualities that can be attributed to my father.

The very interesting thing is that my dad left my mother, me and my sisters when I was 14 and I have not seen him since. I find it fascinating that I admire qualities of someone that hurt my mother when I was growing up, someone that was not there for me, someone I was not able to make a strong connection with. However, this is the person that I admire so much, and I wish I was more like him.

Meanwhile, my mother is one of the most loving and beautiful souls on this planet. If I ever have children and I can be at least half of the amazing mother, she was for me and my sisters I can feel my job as a mum is done. She is someone with the heart of gold and so much love towards everyone that crosses her path, but she also has the qualities that I think are stopping me from living the life I want.

There is a process that I follow with my clients. I call it the *Unf**k Yourself Journey*. It is one of the best steps you can take towards your healing process. No matter how much your parents loved you they f**ked you up. They did the best they could with what they had and knew, but it's very likely they were f**ked up themselves by their own parents. And the vicious cycle goes on. It is your responsibility to get out of it by finding out who you truly are.

Whether you have your money blocks, struggle with intimacy or rejection, cannot commit, suffer from addictions and low self-esteem, or maybe you lack a sense of direction, you will find an answer towards your healing journey. Start by completing *Queen's Awareness* exercise. If you would like to go deeper contact me at WhyAmIStillSingleBook.com

---

Exercise: *Queen's Awareness*

Write down the type of people and their qualities that you admire and find exciting and then ones you find off-putting, unattractive and dull.

When you are done completing your list, look at the list and try to trace back the qualities of people that really loved you in the past or the ones that you loved. See if you can find out anything about yourself.

_____

_____

_____

_____

_____

_____

_____

_____

4. Disney Was Wrong

I love stories. I'm very lucky. I grew up with bedtime stories read by my mum and my aunties. I would also go to my grandmother and she would always tell me stories. She is the best story teller that I know. I remember being a little girl and thinking how one day I'm going to find my magical prince and he will rescue me and then we will have the happy ever after.

What I find interesting about all the stories I was told growing up and everything that Disney wanted me to swallow and believe in is that they never say what happens after you find your prince charming. What does happen after he rescues you and you get married?

If you've ever been in a relationship you probably know that there is so much more than just love and roses, gold and horses. Not that I have ever had any of that in any of my relationships. Oh wait, I think I had it all, except for the horse. Putting that on my list as we speak. NOW!

It has taken me half of the time I have lived on this planet to realise that I don't have to be rescued and I can be my own kind of Queen. I can create my own life. I can do things on my own and I will meet my prince charming one day. He will be by my side and we will complement each other. But I don't have to be rescued, because I can do things for myself being a woman that dances with wolves. You might be thinking: but where is he? One thing at a time. I will cover that. I promise.

Let's go back to how you understand love. Have you ever sat down and thought about your idea of a great relationship? How do you know that what you want in a relationship is something coming from your core values and wishes and not something your environment, your family or your friends are forcing on you based on their own experiences and beliefs?

As much as I would like to think of myself as a smart, sophisticated young lady, an independent thinker, who is able to form her own values and beliefs, I would be lying if I did not admit that Hollywood, Disney, love stories and novels have shaped my idea of what love and a happy relationship is all about.

Another example is *Fifty Shades of Grey* and the whole trilogy of this goodness. Don't you think it is so interesting how so many tickets were sold out before the actual movie came out? I have to be honest, I refused to watch it initially when it came out.

Then I wrote my book for men *How To Get Laid Now.* I was like: you know what, let me go and watch these films and see what it is so special about them. Let me get some ideas for my posts and my Facebook lives. Strictly for research reasons only. Obviously!

And here I was in the comfort of my own bed, dressed in my fluffy pink dressing gown munching on the sweet and salty popcorn. And yes, some parts made me cringe, others made me blush or wonder where I could get one of those Mr Grey creatures myself.

Why do I think *Fifty Shades of Grey* and Mr Grey are rather odd? And no, it has nothing to do with the red room. Did I make it sound that the red room is not odd at all?

Firstly, let's talk about the image of Mr Grey. It shows that nowadays it is not enough for a man to be a millionaire to attract a woman, but he has to be a billionaire. He has to be someone with the thickest stoic mask, but he's also extremely caring. He is someone who has a business worth of billions, but he still has the time to come and spend a spontaneous night or even the whole weekend with his lady. He flies her to places not just first class, but with his own private jet. It's a rather unusual combination.

And yes, it is a rather sexy combination, because not only does he have the best abs and the smoothest moves in bed, but also everything else that you might be dreaming about while coming from another bad date. But how realistic is it?

You might be reading this and thinking that I am putting some unnecessary limitations on you, because men like that do exist. In fact, Mr Grey is exactly someone you would like to find and live the happily ever after.

Don't you think that *Fifty Shades of Grey* is like a grownup Disney story with a modern prince riding a 660-horsepower toy and rescuing a beautiful girl from her misery? And let's not forget he's phenomenal in bed and incredibly well groomed.

Don't get me wrong. Disney stories are great, but do you think you have to be rescued? It is the 21st century and you can be your own woman, the smart, not the angry feminist, someone that owns herself unapologetically. Continue reading if you would like to know how to own your inner Goddess.

For now, please, put your invisible crown and audit that story Disney has sold to you. Let me sprinkle some love dust on you, so you can meet your very own tall, dark, handsome and available.

5. Be Specific

Have you ever been called picky? Let's talk about your wishlist. It's all about him being kind, loving, supportive, funny, hard-working, exciting, driven, adventurous, a great listener . . . that's just to begin with.

Do you want him to be caring and charismatic, someone that can cook and crack the best jokes, intellectual, but laid back, driven and ambitious, but not a workaholic, confident, but not cocky, persistent, but not obsessive, flirty but loyal? Do any of these tick your boxes for Mr Charming?

Exercise. *Queen's Wishlist*

Take a piece of paper or your notebook, you will need a lot of space. Write down everything you would like your special someone to be. Be as specific as you can. Some ideas what you can include.

Religion,
Lifestyle,
Habits,
Career,

Hobbies,
Character,
Eye colour,
The sense of style,
Diet,
Gym habits,
Income,
Stocks/shares,
Pets,
Children,
Home,
Siblings,
Height.

It should take you a few pages to write your wishlist. Be as specific as you can. So specific that you even mention how he likes his tea/coffee, whether he is a cat lover or hater and the breed of his dog. Take time to write the most honest, extremely needy and as unrealistic wishlist as you can think of. Something so embarrassing that you'd probably be hospitalised if someone found out about it.

I want you to do it now. Stop reading this book, take a pen and a piece of paper and start making your list. Take action. NOW. Go go go!

This is how this book was born. I was just sitting at the restaurant in Sicily, brainstorming about my future and what I would like to do with my life and then I had this moment of epiphany. 'You know what? I think I'm ready to write a book for women!'

Then I put a post on Facebook saying how I was going to do that in 24 hours and now you are a witness of that. At the time I was doing this it's 3:20 AM in the morning and I'm just sitting outside under a palm tree. I can hear some birds chirping. I've just looked up and there are stars in the sky. An idyllic scene. The joys of now.

Exercise. *Queen's Wishlist.* **Part II.**

Sit down in a place where you won't be disturbed. Read your list very carefully. Focus on everything that you listed.

Cross out everything you wrote that doesn't make you feel passionate and excited. The things that you are not that bothered about. Only leave those points that you feel excited about.

Put that aside for a minute. Then read it again. Make sure you know that this list has only things that make you feel excited when you are reading it and thinking about this person being your future person.

Keep this list in your drawer next to your bed and read it every other night just before falling asleep. Then wait for the magic to happen.

A disclaimer. In order to attract a quality person, you have to make sure you are a woman of high quality. Do you have what it takes?

If you don't believe you are good enough to attract this person, continue reading this book. You will find a solution.

You will have the tools helping you to Embrace your inner Goddess and how to become a woman that dances with wolves. I am so excited to be on this journey with you.

6. Unrealistic Expectations

I've been dating for more than a decade. I've been in situations where I feel like Charlotte from Sex and the City. Have you ever seen that episode? Charlotte is having a breakfast with her girls trying to recover after a rather wild night out and she says in frustration: 'I've been dating since I was fifteen. I'm exhausted. Where is he?'

Have you ever felt like that? Have you been in that situation where you are told by your family, your friends, your loved ones that you have unrealistic expectations and that you want something impossible. That you are extremely picky and that someone you want does not exist.

Have you ever felt that you could live with almost anyone? You could create your life and you might have even met someone that you could have been happy with. Well, to an extent. However, there are certain things that you crave.

For example, he does not necessarily have to be George Clooney's younger brother with perfectly defined abs and Richards Branson's wealth. What you really crave is the connection. The connection where you are sitting with that person at 3 in the morning laughing, sharing ideas and dreams. You are looking for someone that you can learn from. You are looking for someone that you can be proud of.

You do want to be proud of his achievements and his mind, but more than anything you want to feel proud, because you are next to an incredibly kind person. Also, someone that you catch sometimes looking at you like you look at that pizza when you have been waiting at the restaurant for 30 minutes and it is finally here. But the feeling is mutual. Because you know, that pizza could care less how excited you are to see or taste it.

I have a story to tell you. I came back from my backpacking trip. I spent 9 months travelling and volunteering in Southeast Asia. You will find out more about that later. Also, I will give you some travel tips if you would like to have your own Indiana Jones experience.

Here I am back in the UK after 9 months of living out of a backpack and being a free spirit full of sand in my hair and Vietnamese coffee running through my veins. I just had this feeling that I was ready to settle down. I felt that I was ready to stay in one place. What I didn't realise was that my staying in one place was more like staying in the same town or country and not living from my backpack. It meant being able to cook my own breakfast and keep my cookies for as long as I want in the cupboard without worrying that aunts or rats will munch on them. I did not understand that settling down wasn't about meeting a guy who asked me on the second date if I wanted children or in what kind of house I would like to live.

Has it ever happened to you that you wish for something and then you realise it was not what you wanted? It has happened to me. I know I have to be careful what I wish for. Whether it's positive or negative. I am a big believer in the law of attraction. Not the one where you are running in your garden screaming to get your leads, but the one where you make things happen with your thoughts and actions. I include that in one of my training sessions that my clients really enjoy. Always have lots of fun doing it.

Let's go back to the story. To be continued in the third person.

Ieva met an amazing guy. She did not think much of him to begin with, but he was so different compared to the tall, handsome, unavailable she was more used to having around. He admired her. He looked at her with those hungry pizza eyes. He thought Ieva was amazing and would always tell her that. He said she was beautiful, smart, intelligent, funny and insanely sexy.

He was always on time. He planned and arranged the next date after dropping her home. It was so unknown for Ieva and a bit strange. Just too good to be true. Also, her tummy was reacting in a funny way every time he started talking children and the real estate.

He brought her coffee in bed and picked up freshly baked croissants from the local bakery. He introduced her to all his friends and his parents. They even started thinking about having business together.

After 9 months of knowing each other they moved in together. Ieva would still get that funny tummy feeling, but everyone around her kept reminding her what a great catch he was. Everyone was so happy for her. But she wasn't sure. Ieva just couldn't stay up with him till 3 in the morning watching the stars.

He did not know what to do. He thought he gave all he had. Ieva thought he gave too much and she had no idea what to do with all that.

The day she made the decision to move out, the funny feeling in her tummy was gone. She called her mum to say how happy she was. Her mum did not see it that way. She said her daughter would regret this mistake for the rest of her life.

This is an example of what happens when you buy into the idea that you have unrealistic expectations. This also comes from a lack of self-awareness and not knowing who you truly are. Don't feel guilty for stepping away from something you feel is not right for you. Instead, move away from the situation that does not fulfil you. Guess what? The person you are holding on to for no reason is someone's unrealistic expectation.

I am not a believer in THE ONE concept and I am going to talk about it later. But if you are currently dating and something just does not feel right for you it might be the right time to look deep into yourself and what you really want. Treat others the way you would like to be treated, my darling.

You do not have to change your hair, your ways or become a completely different person to feel that you deserve to be loved and appreciated. You are enough.

Ieva K.

CHAPTER II

You Are the Goddess

1. You Are Enough

Have you ever tried to change your ways and who you are, because of that special someone? Have you ever heard him say that he loves when you add more salt into the pasta you cook for him? He says he prefers when your hair is straight. He wants you to wear your heels instead of those ballerinas. He doesn't really like that your underwear is not matching, and he would rather see you wear something that Victoria's Secret angels have on their perfect little bodies. He tells you your best friend is no good. He says she is too full of herself.

I would like to think of myself as an independent, sophisticated, smart and intelligent young lady. I have a secret. It is something I have never told anyone before.

I have been in situations where I would adjust myself just to please him. Here's an example for you, so you can get a better idea about Ieva, the man pleaser, and maybe you will even have your own aha moment.

First things first. If you have never met me before and you only know me from this book I would like you to know a couple of things about Ieva. I am a bubbly person. I love talking to strangers and asking 'why'. I love knowing why people do what they do. I love learning from people. That's one of the reasons why I do what I do as an author, lifestyle and relationship coach. I have learned so much from my clients. And I am learning every single day, but when it comes to me, I can be blind sometimes. And that is the reason why you do need a coach, my darling.

> *Ieva is seeing this guy. One of those tall, handsome and unavailable. They are having a lovely chat while sipping their tea. He tells her how he was at the local coffee shop earlier and this guy told him that he was talking to her. Then he tells Ieva it is not such a good idea for her to speak to strangers, especially men.*
>
> *He tells her that this man is just after her pussy and that he is getting the wrong idea. He himself understands that Ieva is just being friendly, but that strange man thinks that she is flirting. She is easy and too available. He loves and respects her too much and he does not want anyone to treat her that way. Next thing you know Ieva is apologizing for talking to that guy.*

What do you think about this?

Do you want me to tell you what I think? I want to take this girl, shake her a little, and then pour a bucket of iced water on her hoping she would come to her senses. And the most interesting thing is that this girl was no one else, but me. It has been five years since this incident. Today I know better than that, but back then I did not.

You might be in a completely different situation. You might be with someone who is being physically abusive towards you. You were able to convince yourself that this is all you deserve and now you cannot even imagine that it can be different. You might even think it's your fault he gets upset with you, because of the way you are. And you should know better than that.

That's why I am writing this book. I want you to see that you are not alone. I might have not had someone punch me in the face, but I was able to abuse myself with my thoughts and I spent too much time around people that did not see the magic in me. And the only reason for that was because I did not think I was enough. I did not think that my own light was important enough. Please, seek support if you cannot come to your senses yourself. I would be more than happy to help you. Contact me at WhyAmIStill SingleBook.com

Don't be around someone that makes you feel you are not good enough. If you love talking to people you continue talking to people. If you love having tasteless food, you do that. If he wants more salt or pepper he can always add it himself. You do not have to change your hair, your ways or become a completely different person to feel that you deserve to be loved and appreciated. You are enough.

> **TIP**
>
> *How to look after your inner Goddess?*
>
> Put a sticky note on all the mirrors around your house with the words 'You are enough'.
>
> Set a reminder on your phone that tells you a couple of times a day 'You are enough'.
>
> Every single time you see that note or the reminder take a moment to say one good thing about yourself. It could be anything. From your cooking skills, to your beautiful eyes, your gorgeous smile or maybe how good you are at petting your cat.
>
> Do it for 30 days and tell me what you have noticed. I dare you.
>
> Even if you do not do it, YOU ARE ENOUGH. You deserve love.

2. 90-60-90

Do you know what 90-60-90 stands for? I have not heard of this in a long time, because the beauty standards change almost as often as the hairstyles. One day you are the most desirable if you have a flat chest and look like a boy. The next day you must have breasts and a bottom like Kim Kardashian.

If you have no idea what 90-60-90 stand for I shall educate you. It is the supposed measurements (in centimetres) of a perfect woman, measured at the bust, waist and hips.

When I was a little girl I would watch *FashionTV* and

I would admire models walking on the catwalk thinking how perfect they were. Also, there would be model editions presenting in detail every model. From their star sign, hair and eye colour, to the size of their bust, waist and hips. I would watch them mesmerised admiring their beauty and assets.

I remember looking at those measurements 90-60-90, and thinking of it as the perfect body. Before I jump into the climax of this story, I want you to keep in mind that my brain at that point was the size of a peanut. Also, when it comes to my body I've never been a big girl. On the contrary, I have always been quite slim. When I was a teenager I was awkwardly skinny. I think I was the last girl in my class to get breasts. The more I think about it I realise that most of those busty girls just had well padded bras. But I didn't know these things back then. I would always look at curvy girls wondering why I wasn't one of them.

Let's go back to 90-60-90. Imagine a 14-year-old Ieva standing in front of the mirror and wrapping a measuring tape around her to see if her body meets the 90-60-90 criteria. What do you think? My chest was way less than 90 centimetres. I think even today it is less than that. I remember my tummy was just around 60 centimetres. My hips were rather far off. I remember standing there and thinking my body was not good enough, because I did not fit into the measurements of a perfect woman. I remember thinking I was not beautiful, because my body was not 90-60-90.

What did I do? I started doing some exercises to flatten my belly. I would do them after school or whenever I would have some spare time. I do not know for how long I did it. Probably, a week or so. I remember wrapping the measuring tape around me to track my progress. I was lucky, because I got distracted by something else. It could be that I have simply come into the realization that I am not a model. But you might be someone who has developed an eating disorder while exercising similar practices. I will talk about it later.

You are a grown-up, smart woman. You look at magazines, social media posts, Instagram girls and wonder how they all look so perfect. Their perfect skin and cellulite free toned thighs. When a 14-year-old girl starts doing sit-ups and crunches to get a slimmer waist to fit the beauty standards set by fashion houses to save on a fabric, it sounds funny, but also extremely sad.

What about a grownup woman who is more likely to read an article telling her how to keep her breasts looking amazing instead of clicking on a post that teaches how to get an inner peace? I am guilty of doing that.

As I got a bit older and wiser, I started to love myself more. I'm someone that sleeps naked and has a full-size mirror in the bedroom. When I wake up I look at myself. Yeah that's TMI, but I feel like you and I are sisters by now. Some days I feel like I am a piece of art. Then I give myself that powerful superwoman's look. On the days when I feel far from the goddess, I just tell myself that my eyes are lying, because the day before I was shining.

As cheesy as it is, you're beautiful just the way you are. I know that about myself even if there are bits I am not a fan of. If you could just see yourself through the eyes of your lover. The lover that wants to get lost in every inch of your body. The lover that wants to make love to you with all the lights switched on. The lover that makes you feel that you are the most beautiful girl in the world. Guess what? You can have those eyes yourself. You just have to see how absolutely amazing you are. Respect your body for what it is capable of. This body is so much more than just silly numbers.

Exercise. *You Are the Goddess.*

Sit comfortably where you are not interrupted. Take a deep breath. Breathe in through your nose, breathe out through your mouth. Close your eyes.

Have a feel of all the different parts of your body. Go from your face to your neck, from your finger tips to your elbows, from your tummy to your thighs.

Take time to think about all the things you can do thanks to your body.

Think about your legs and the places they have taken you. Think about your hands and the handshakes you have given with them. Think about your arms and all the amazing hugs.

Take a moment to think about your body for what it is capable of and all the gifts it has given to you. Feel that within your body. Your body is your temple. Your body is a masterpiece. You are enough. Take a deep breath in and out. Repeat the breathing till the count of ten.

If you would like to do this meditation with me, you can find a guided You Are the Goddess meditation on my website WhyAmIStillSingleBook.com

3. Cake Over Lettuce

I am a very lucky girl. I have never been on a slimming diet. I've been on a diet where I tried not to eat any processed sugar and cut down my dairy intake to clear out my skin. However, I've never been on a diet trying to lose weight. Not even when I stayed in Italy for 6 months and my ex-boyfriend would feed me pasta at 10PM. That gave me some extra belly fat.

However, I've never had an eating disorder. Some interesting facts I have come across while researching the topic:

'Over 1.6 million people in the UK are estimated to be directly affected by eating disorders. This is likely to be an underestimate as we know there is a huge level of unmet need in the community. Good quality comprehensive services for people with eating disorders are not yet available in many parts of England.'[2]

It also states that a more realistic figure is closer to 4 million as the majority of people affected by eating disorders do not seek help.

If I am in a group of ladies, who, no matter how sophisticated, smart, and educated they are, sooner or later at least a couple will mention their body concerns. It is usually weight loss related. I am aware these are completely different cases when someone just wants to lose weight before that sunny get away and when someone hugs a toilet after every meal or

---

2 Statistics, 2017, Anorexia & Bulimia Care, http://www.anorexi abulimiacare.org.uk/about/statistics

survives on one grape a day. But how often do we, women, shame each other about our weight?

If you are a big girl and order the biggest meal at McDonalds, people are judging, thinking they know the reason behind your figure. If you are a big girl and order just salad, some might say you are faking it, because you can't really look like that eating just lettuce.

If you are a skinny girl and you are eating your salad, people make comments saying they are not surprised you are this skinny if that is all you are surviving on. If you are having a double cheeseburger people say you are just pretending to be eating this much. Once you are alone you starve yourself. No matter what you do, someone will criticize you. You might as well do whatever you want.

I was watching Marisa Peer, one of the best British Therapists, talk about her online weight loss program and she said something that has really stayed with me: 'You are not what you eat. You are what you think.'[3]

This makes so much sense to me. I think of myself as someone who has a pretty good relationship with food. I say it based on the women I see around, and women I grew up with. I remember when I was 8 years old I would play a game with my auntie where I had to watch her all day and make sure she did not eat anything. My mum would eat some odd cabbage thing and nothing else for the whole week in order to fit into her special dress.

I am not scared of food and I have never been. I have

---

3 Marisa Peer, 2015, Perfect Weight Forever by Marisa Peer, https://www.youtube.com/watch?v=fWXmaLpluOg&t=1047s

this deep belief in myself that it is OK if I have that piece of cake or that chocolate bar. Nothing wrong with that. But I am not going to have it all the time, because I want to look after my body, my beautiful temple, my powerhouse. I think it deserves more nutritious food. I can open a packet of crisps and leave half of it in the cupboard after I have felt I had enough. Yes, I do have some crazy cravings at that time of the month or if I feel a bit meh, but they do not last for long

I have been in a position where I was eating sugary things trying to mask my inner pain. Once, I remember standing in Tesco and going through the sweets aisle. Picking up some chocolate desserts, getting home and eating all four at once while binge watching KUWTK. If you have no idea what this stands for I am hoping you won't be trying to Google it. If you do. Oh well, now you know.

I remember being in bed and watching myself from the distance and just thinking, 'What is this? I wonder, what is hurting inside of you?' I bet it was something more like, 'You are such a failure. You are concentrating too much on your pain. Stop feeling sorry for yourself. Go and do something with your life'. But that's not something Ieva would say today. She knows better. Hence, she speaks to herself with words filled with kindness. Most of the time.

I want to introduce you to someone very special. A girl that means the world to me. Let me call her Alice. I am only borrowing her story. I know one day she will tell it herself, but she is not ready yet.

Alice was an incredibly happy girl when growing up. She loved her food a lot. She was one of those kids that had

a great appetite. Alice was a real trouble maker. Slightly a tomboy. She grew up playing with cars. She loved to construct things. She is a girl of many talents. When she was seven her parents got a divorce. No one explained to her what was happening.

When she reached her early teens, she developed a tummy condition. She could not eat certain foods. Her mum tried so many things, took her to a number of doctors trying to figure out what was the problem behind Alice's tummy ache.

One summer Alice got so slim. Everyone was complimenting her. She felt so good. They said she looked like a model. She could see that even boys started paying attention to her.

Fast forward a little, Alice tried to kill herself. Fortunately, she failed. Her family found out there was nothing wrong with her tummy. She had been battling bulimia and anorexia for too many years.

Alice could not do anything about her parents getting a divorce, but she thought she could at least be in control of what her body looked like. She has always been extremely determined and hardworking, so sticking to that had never been a problem. Today she focuses on other things. She focuses on building her empire.

Recently she had the first symptoms of body dysmorphia. She got scared. She sought help. She did not want to be in that scary place she was years ago. Alice says it is all about noticing when those days are coming and asking for help instead of trying to battle it alone. I hope you listen to Alice.

I hope you ask for help. Whatever is hurting you, it can be healed. You are worthy of love no matter what size or shape you are. You deserve to meet the person that will absolutely adore you. But there is one tiny thing. You have to be your own biggest cheerleader first.

You are a beautiful Goddess. A gift to this world. Do not dim your light. And if you are hurting, please, seek help. I would love to support you on this journey. Get in touch. WhyAmIStillSingleBook.com

---

Exercise: *You Are Beautiful.*

Write down 10 things that you really like about your appearance. It can be anything. From that beauty spot next to your elbow to your gorgeous feet.

Once you are done writing take a moment to really admire yourself.

1. _____

2. _____

3. _____

4. _____

5. _____

6. _____

7. _____

8. _____

9. _____

10. _____

4. Boss Lady Mindset

I am a big believer that if I put my mind, hard work and lots of determination into something I can achieve almost anything I want. However, I have noticed when coaching others, I truly believe they can reach the stars, but when it comes to myself, I often doubt it. Very often I make myself smaller. I tell myself I can't do certain things. Even while writing this book I have to reassure myself all the time that it is good enough, I have something to say and I hope you, dear Goddess, are finding it useful.

I think this also stems from my childhood. When I was growing up I was surrounded by educated, intelligent, elegant, sophisticated women, but none of them were too career driven. I would have never thought of myself as a future business owner, author, and authority.

However, when I got slightly older I started thinking about my own definition of success.

When I put myself away from my usual surroundings and when I surround myself with the right people and knowledge I can see how ideas are just flowing at me and I see what is available out there. It's very simple.

If you are surrounded by girls and women who get wages that are slightly above the minimum, you are more likely to think that this is a normal standard available for you. On the other hand, if your friends are successful business owners or highly paid professionals, you start thinking: 'How come I don't have this? Let me see what they do. Let me learn from them.'

Another important point to mention, you might think that certain things are not available for you just because you are a woman. You were not brought up like that boy living next door. He learned to compete at a very early age. You were mainly competing with other girls about your looks. You were conditioned not to be too much. You were conditioned to be a people pleaser. You might have even been told not to have ambitions that are too big as they might prevent you from having a husband.

'What if both boys and girls were raised not to link masculinity and money? What if their attitude was not "the boy has to pay," but rather, "whoever has more should pay'. Of course, because of their historical advantage, it is mostly men who will have more today. But if we start raising children differently, then in fifty years, in a hundred years, boys will no longer have the pressure of proving their masculinity by material means.

But by far the worst thing we do to males—by making them feel they have to be hard—is that we leave them with very fragile egos. The harder a man feels compelled to be, the weaker his ego is.

And then we do a much greater disservice to girls, because we raise them to cater to the fragile egos of males.

We teach girls to shrink themselves, to make themselves smaller.

We say to girls: You can have ambition, but not too much. You should aim to be successful but not too successful, otherwise you will threaten the man. If you are the breadwinner in your relationship with a man, *pretend that you are not, especially in public, otherwise you will emasculate him.'*[4]

I want to introduce you to a bad ass woman, Mel Robbins. She is a serial entrepreneur, author, one of the most booked motivational speakers in the world. I really love this woman. When I watch her videos, I feel like fire.

I was trying to get her write a foreword for my book. I did everything I could think of. Twitter, Facebook, Instagram, email. More than once. Got an email with a no. Then I put notifications to know when Mel posted on her Instagram and started commented on all her posts. Finally, managed to make another contact. She commented saying she was proud of my achievements but had too many things going on. Oh well. At least I tried.

There is a very interesting interview I want you to have a little glimpse at. During her interview with Success Magazine Mel Robbins is asked why women don't get ahead. Mel starts by mentioning Harvard Business school's study during which they asked a great number of managers what the number one reason was that they were not promoting their female staff members. Guess what was the answer? They all thought she lacked confidence for the new role.

Mel Robbins gives a very simple tip how to appear more confident during a business meeting. Instead of slouching and diving into taking thorough notes, record the conversation on your phone and then listen to it. Or

---

4 Chimamanda Ngozi Adichie, 2012, *We Should All be Feminists.* Vintage Books

just use an app to have it transcribed. Sit back, relax and be present. And the most important thing—do not leave the meeting room without asking a question. If you are not comfortable with that just comment on someone else's idea giving positive feedback.

Another very simple way to look more confident is to start sending emails that sound more assertive and straight to the point. Stop rambling and explaining yourself.[5]

Every single day you have these great ideas coming to you like shooting stars. I remember when I put all over my social media that I was writing this book just to make sure I stuck to it. I woke up the next morning thinking it was the worst idea ever, but I decided to do it anyway. Imagine if I hadn't?

Your ideas are important. It is not about who is the most talented, the most gifted, who has the best body or is the smartest in the room. It's all about whether you are an action taker or not. That is what being a boss is all about. Do you let yourself take risks and make mistakes or not? I am typing this as a reminder for myself. I am worthy. I know I can do it.

You can have it all. You can have a great career, business, and a great relationship. Please, do not limit yourself based on what you see around you. You can create your own life. You are great the way you are today, and you deserve all the goodness in the world. Start implementing small changes today and you will be surprised what you can achieve and

---

5   Success Magazine, 2017, Mel Robbins: This is Why Women Don't Get Ahead, https://www.youtube.com/watch?v=2ADB_H3Bi_I

how liberating it feels when you finally take action towards that boss lady life.

5. Stop Scrolling

Raise your hand if you are guilty of scrolling through your Instagram or Facebook and wondering why do these people have everything? Why does everyone seem to have their shit together but me? Everyone is going to these amazing places. How are they able to do these big things in life? I could get those abs, but I lose my motivation before I start even doing it. How are they able to achieve so much? And I'm just here living the most boring life. I know I could do better. I see people that are not even that smart achieve so much. I should be doing better. I don't think I believe I can be great. There's no point even trying.

Raise your hand if you've felt that way? You have been working towards something for a really long time, but you cannot see the progress. Well, not the progress you see Instagram kids share where they are able to earn 6 figures just by being on their phones for a few hours a day. And then you think you might as well not do anything at all. You end up in bed for a few days watching Netflix. Chilling and eating bad food, feeling sorry for yourself. Then you pick yourself up.

But the truth is you are in this vicious cycle. You cannot help your scrolling. You compare yourself to others. You compare your body, your income, your life achievements, your relationship status with someone you don't even know that well. You do not know what is behind that big smile and perfectly orchestrated image.

Have you ever thought that you might be comparing someone's chapter 20 with your chapter 2? Pat yourself on the back for what you have already accomplished. I know it might not be easy if you are an overachiever or a driven, ambitious lady that has the highest standards when it comes to her own performance. But I am sure you are doing your very best as long as you are learning and going forward while enjoying the stillness and indulging in the most precious NOW.

I want to share something personal. I am writing this book sitting under a palm tree in Sicily. Feeling extremely blessed. You would not believe where I was this time last month. I was in a mental hospital.

How did it all happen?

After writing my book *How to Get Laid Now* I went all in building my coaching business. I was watching Gary V and hustling and doing jab jab jab. I was feeding myself with quotes like 'It doesn't matter where you are now, it is all about where you can be tomorrow', 'be obsessed about what you do', 'you can sleep when you die' and so on.

I neglected my feminine side, my feminine power. I was trying to be more like a man. I was pushing myself as much as I could. I spent as much time as I could on social media building my following and chatting to people at 2 in the morning. I was collecting likes and getting messages from well-respected business people, but I neglected all the people around me. I felt it was time to move on and build new relationships, because the old ones were not serving me. I isolated myself.

I spent hours online trying to get on someone's podcast when all I really needed was to go with someone for a coffee.

I withdrew myself from everyone and I got lonely. I have a history of mental illness in my family. I have been dealing with the episodes of depression for almost 10 years. But this time it was rather serious. I was feeling suicidal. I was googling things like 'what is the easiest way to kill yourself' and 'how to overdose', 'ways to kill yourself so it looks like an accident'.

If I didn't have someone that knew I wasn't right I do not think I would be writing this book. I do not think I would still be here. I was in a very dark place. I felt nothing, I wanted nothing. Then I would push myself to get out of bed and do a high energy Facebook live, because when I scrolled through my feed it was all about that hustle.

You are a human being and it is incredibly important to progress in life. You were put here for a reason. But you cannot help others if you are hurting yourself. Your light is the most important. You cannot find love if you are not filled with love. And there's only one you.

When I was going through my mental health challenge a friend of mine told me, 'The biggest souls sometimes have to go through the biggest challenges.'

If you're going through something similar you probably do not feel like the biggest soul. You are more likely to feel like a black hole. But you know what? It is not forever. This is your illness talking. I promise. Find someone you can talk to about this. You can overcome it. It will go away if you work on it. Not in a jab jab jab kind of way, but in the way filled with the most beautiful feminine power and love. Love for yourself.

Getting to know yourself journey is a life-long process. I dream that one day there is a special scanner that you walk through and it tells you if you are ready for a relationship or whether it is better to invest more time and energy into your personal growth.

Scrolling through Instagram and comparing yourself with someone's perfectly staged life is normal and it is something that most of us do, but it is not something that will help you grow. Watch yourself through the day and notice how you react to what you see on the screen. Try to limit your time on the screen. And always remember that it is ok to unfollow someone who does not make you feel that your heart is filled with love.

6. Morning / Night Routine

If you have ever met me in person or have seen my social media posts, you might be surprised to find out about my battle with depression. I remember when I told my friend that I was at the mental hospital. Her words, 'You are one of the happiest and full of life people that I know in my life. How is that even possible?'

These things can happen to anyone. If you are a high achiever, someone who is always striving for more, you might be neglecting yourself and your health. It is so important that you embrace your feminine side and fill your cup first. Take time for yourself. Check in with yourself before checking in with the world. What do you want? I promise, those emails and messages are still going to be there. By taking time for yourself you will be in a better state of mind to handle whatever the world or your inbox throws at you. Look after yourself. I don't want you to get in the place of exhaustion and complete inner emptiness that I was facing. I did not put myself first.

One of the most important things to remember—you are the most important person on this planet. Whether you are a single girl, a mum, an auntie or someone's carer, you cannot take care of anyone else if you have not taken care of yourself.

The most successful people, whatever success means to you, have a morning routine. Some of them meditate, others listen to the same song for 30 minutes, read, do mindfulness exercises, yoga stretches, write a gratitude diary, have a cold shower, run around the block.

No matter what you do first thing in the morning, it has to be all about you. Check in with yourself before you jump into the world and everyone's requests. You cannot love anyone if your own love glass is empty.

Start by asking yourself these simple questions before you get out of bed.

1. What am I grateful for this morning?
2. What could make this day great?
3. Who is the person that I can send some love vibes to?
4. How am I feeling? What can I do to feel (even) better?
5. What am I proud of?

Your day will be so much better if you just take a moment to answer one of those questions before getting out of bed. You are setting an intention instead of checking how well your recent post did. You are treating yourself with love and care. Your body and mind will thank you for that.

My morning routine (when it actually happens):

I wake up after pressing snooze too many times. On a good day I do a very quick yoga stretch watching one of *Yoga with Adriene* videos on YouTube. It is usually just for 7 minutes or so. Then I have a glass of water if I remembered to bring it in to my bedroom the night before. I always have a shower. Once I am back from the shower I listen to something positive/spiritual, sometimes more motivational while I am getting ready. I continue to listen to it while I am having my breakfast. I never skip breakfast. I cannot do anything if I don't eat my breakfast.

Disclaimer: I have not done this thorough routine in a couple of weeks. I had a man staying around. It has messed up my morning routine. I stay in bed for too long. But I have been colouring before diving into any kind of work. I love it. It makes me feel relaxed and it helps me to get into the right state of mind.

Whether I am doing my morning routine or not there is one rule I always follow, and it has helped me massively. I do not check my phone for the first hour.

I have muted all my notifications on the phone. When I go on YouTube while I am getting ready for the day I do not see any notifications. If I don't do that I start feeling anxious and frustrated. I have learned that the hard way, but it has been one of the best things I have done for myself and my wellbeing. Check in with yourself before you check in with the world.

I am also working on improving what I do before going to bed. Ideally, I would not want to be online two hours before my bedtime. I would like to read for 30 minutes, write a few lines in my diary. I have succeeded at some of it. But I want to do better than that. There are nights when I am checking my Facebook or Instagram feed just before going to bed. But I never fall asleep next to my phone. I charge it away from my bed. You should too.

I know you understand the importance of being in the most harmonious relationship with yourself. It is never going to be just love and roses, but you can try your best. When you are in a beautiful loving relationship with yourself it is much easier to be in a healthy relationship with other people. Take care of yourself in order to attract and invite love into your life.

Exercise: *Queen's Habits*

Create your own morning/night routine. It can be anything you want it to be. It does not have to be anything out of this world. Just something simple.

What is that one thing you can start doing first thing in the morning to have a better day?

_____

_____

_____

_____

_____

_____

_____

Find someone that does not feel emasculated by your greatness but celebrates and cherishes it instead by feeling proud to wake up next to a lady like you.

Ieva K.

CHAPTER III

Where Is He?

1. The Red Dress

I know I know. Red symbolises passion, love, desire. I am sure you know it all. However, it is very likely red is not a colour easily found in your wardrobe. It might even be that it is so out of your comfort zone that you would never even dream of wearing something red.

Do you wear a red lipstick? When you are conquering the world and all you see around are mainly ladies dressed in dark colours and here you are with something completely different, it draws the attention towards you. It makes a big difference in how you feel about yourself, the vibrations and the message you send to the world. I'm not telling you to wear a red Bodycon dress going to a meeting or while you are doing your grocery shopping, but I would like to encourage you to introduce more colours into your wardrobe.

Have you ever worn a red dress? It does not even have to be one of those short tiny dresses. No matter what length or cut it is. If you have ever worn a red dress, you will agree that it has some magical powers. People are drawn to you. You are more flirty than usual, you feel more alive. Ok, maybe that's just me. But I know red always works.

When I wrote my first book and I was mostly working with men, I strategically put the hot red on my cover. I strategically wore red nail vanish during events. I strategically changed my profile picture to the one where I am wearing a red top and a red lip. It draws the attention. On a couple of occasions, I had men contacting me just because they were drawn to that red.

Indeed, very often it is not the attention I would like to receive. My inbox gets flooded with dick pics and dick videos. Recently I received an audio recording, where it is obvious that the sender is in the middle of some serious matter. Don't you worry. I educate men about this kind of unsolicited footage all the time.

Anyway, going back to the red. If your wardrobe is not the most colourful have a little bit of fun with it. Get some bright shoes, a beautiful top that makes your eyes pop and a dress that shows your figure. It is ok to embrace your gorgeous feminine side and have fun being a woman. There is a reason why a woman is the inspiration behind the most beautiful pieces of art. You are gorgeous. Don't hide it.

You do not have to make yourself less. If you are a busty lady show your girls when it is appropriate. If you have the legs to die for don't hide them in those jeans. No matter what body type or shape you have don't dim your light.

I know being in a male dominated business environment sometimes makes you feel that you have to dress in a certain way in order to be perceived in a serious way. Can you relate? There is something very special I want to share with you.

A friend of mine sent me a video. It was one of those videos by *The Daily Goalcast* with dramatic music and inspirational words. But this one was different. I saw a lady speak who got my attention within the first few seconds. She was fierce and fearless. I was mesmerised.

I had an urge to contact her just to say how much I loved her *The Too Much Woman* speech. Guess what? I looked her up on Facebook and I messaged her. Gina Hatzis replied to my message. She thanked for my kind words. I asked her if I could use an extract from her speech in my book. I told her how inspiring I found it. Make sure you check out this beautiful soul and #TooMuchWomanMovement.

'We are not a piece of human. We are not flesh, ass and temptation. We are feminine energy with masculine force. We are sexy brilliance and we are hot determination. We are bigger than our breasts and more powerful than our thighs and our curve is mightier than any sword, and our wit stronger than any insult. We are not here to radiate, to taunt you, to provoke, to threaten you. We shine not for your adoration: we shine, because, baby, you just can't dim the sun.[6]

I wrote this book, because I want you to love yourself before looking for that someone special to make you feel loved. I wrote this book because I want to do everything I can to make sure you don't dim your sun and your fire. I want you to see how amazing you are.

---

6 Gina Hatzis, 2018, *The Too Much Woman*, https://m.facebook. com/story.php?story_fbid=2044696289118780&id=13992060 47001144

You have to find what works the best for you. Sometimes it might help if you just put on a red lipstick. Sometimes you might need to dance naked in front of the full-size mirror unleashing your inner Beyoncé. Whatever it takes. Do it. You are fire.

Exercise. *Red Queen*

Think of the ways you can brighten up your wardrobe. Make the use of that bright blouse you bought ages ago, but had no chance to wear.

If you just finished reading this part of the book and are thinking you could never wear something that draws attention to you, especially, not the colour red, think of the reasons behind it.

Why don't you enjoy being at the centre of attention?

Take a few minutes to journal about it. I would love to hear what you have learned about yourself. Tell me by contacting me on WhyAmIStillSingleBook.com

---

2. Auction Till You Drop

Let me guess. You are reading this title and wondering what an auction has to do with you being single or looking for love. I promise I have a point.

One of the main concerns that I hear from single ladies is 'Where can I meet a quality partner?'

Remember when I told you in *Chapter I* to do the *Queen's Wishlist* exercise where you are writing down everything you want in your ideal partner and then you eliminate things you do not feel passionate about. If you haven't completed your *Queen's Wishlist* do it now. When you become clear about what you want, you start attracting that. But you have to make sure you are not spending your nights watching make-up tutorials.

How can going to an auction help you meet your potential partner? Look at your *Queen's Wishlist* concentrating on his habits and hobbies, his career or business. Think where this person could be hanging out. Where do you think this person would be having his coffee? Does he care about supporting a local business or is he someone who could not care less and is happy to have his coffee from *Starbucks*.

Where do you think this person could be spending his free time? Does he go to the gym? Does he go to the gym to lift or is he more of a swimmer or a sauna lover? Maybe he does yoga. If you are going to the gym that costs **£12.99/** month, it is more likely to be filled with students. Once the price rises, the audience changes.

Would you like to meet someone that loves going to seminars, self-development or investment events? Is he someone who sits at the very back, because he hasn't paid for his ticket? Maybe he is at the very front as a VIP or a platinum ticket holder, sitting as close as possible to the speaker, having VIP lunch and mingling with other VIP guests looking for someone he could have a joint venture with.

Is he someone who goes to auctions hunting for an investment property, or someone who loves going to galleries and live music events, hipster coffee shops and wine tasting nights? Is he an adrenaline junkie or someone that loves to learn about the secrets of meditation?

Also, go to places that are filled with men. A sports bar is perfect for that. I remember going to watch a boxing match with a couple of guys. I entered a sports bar and I could not believe what I saw. The amount of testosterone flying around. Left and right. They were everywhere. It can be a very cheerful and relaxed place as well if the right person or team is winning. All you have to do is look at someone you fancy and smile a couple of times.

You could always meet him at the supermarket or at the bus stop and have the most romantic story to share when people ask how you two met. Sadly, this has never happened to me. I am here to share with you what I know. I am here to share with you what can give you results.

If you are in places where you think your potential partner could be there is something extremely important you have to keep in mind. If you don't take anything else from this book then just take this. Only go to places, only do things, because you want to. Not because you are just looking for that special person.

Have fun and do the things you love. Create something for yourself and your future. Do not place your life on hold putting all your energy and time in finding that person that you could have the happily ever after with.

Once you concentrate on working towards your goals you will see how everything else just falls into place. If you would like to have more clearance when it comes to your personal goals and would love to have someone you can be accountable to, make sure you contact me on WhyAmIStillSingleBook. com. I would love you be part of my *Queen's Club* where you can meet amazing ladies just like you.

A couple of things to keep in mind, so you don't spend

too much time shooting without desirable results. If you are after a rich guy (no judgement, you can have whatever you want) you do not want to go to McDonalds to get your coffee. It makes more sense to go to an expensive hotel that is not far from you. Again, if you cannot think of a hotel that makes great coffee, no love story is worth ruining your relationship with your best friend, that is coffee. Get your priorities right!

Make sure you are not lonely on this journey. Get your tribe to support you. You will find out later about the importance of having your tribe and what happened to me when I neglected my girlfriends. Make sure you have single friends that want to go with you to all the fun places. I don't mind going alone, but I know for some people it is a big NO NO.

Be creative and get specific. No matter what you do remember to have fun. When you are having fun, you are sending magical vibrations into the world. That's when all the big stuff happens. I promise.

Exercise. *Where Kings Hang Out*

Write down 10 places where you think your potential partner could be spending time.

Make a commitment to visit one of those places this week.

1. _____

2. _____

3. _____

4.	_____
5.	_____
6.	_____
7.	_____
8.	_____
9.	_____
10.	_____

3. Write a Book

Do you often get approached by men? I hardly ever get approached by men and this is one of the main reasons why I wrote my book for men *How To Get Laid Now. The Modern Man's Strategy To Approaching Women Like the Boss*. I encourage men through the whole book to go out into the world and talk to women.

Not in a way where they use some cheesy pick up lines, but I encourage them to just go out and have normal fun conversations. Dear Goddess, when was the last time you had a great conversation with a male you didn't know at all that approached you while you were sitting at the coffee shop? Exactly! He hasn't read my book yet.

You will read later about the ways you can be more in charge whether you are meeting a man at a bar or at one of the online dating sites. Don't you think you can do a better job using your own initiative? But that's later. And now, why should you write a book?

I want to share something that happened to me. I thought

it was rather interesting and surprising. I started writing my book and I put an announcement on social media. I shared details of my upcoming book, so people could pre-order. I was rather surprised with the response.

I am not talking about a couple of guys that took it too personally and sent me messages asking me who did I think I was that I could write a book like that. They said they did not need a book like that, because they could get any girl they wanted. Good on you, pal.

I got so many messages from men that I haven't seen or spoken to in ages. They just messaged me saying how cool it was that I was writing a book and that they really admired me for what I was doing. They said I was brave and that it was so attractive that I was doing something so cool. That I was doing something I was passionate about.

Also, I got messages from potential clients saying how they are looking for a woman just like me. They are looking for someone who is a smart, intelligent lady, driven and is working towards her goals. They are looking for someone who does not just stay in a comfortable job, but is doing something she really loves. Someone who likes challenges.

I remember walking down the street in Nottingham and this guy stopped me. Someone that I used to work with. He was with his friend and he introduced me a lady who is writing a book. He looked so excited. He said how amazing and inspirational it was. He congratulated me.

I got messages from random men saying how attractive it was to see a lady going after her dreams and doing something she is so passionate about. And those messages were not creepy at all. They were nice. These men did not even try to flirt or anything. But some of them were married and they would just say how they are trying to inspire their partners do something with their lives, but they could not relate to that.

Do you get my point? Girl, you have to write a book. Ok, you do not necessarily have to write a book, but just do that thing. You know that one thing you have been thinking about for a while. You get these great ideas and these little nuggets of wisdom every single day. That voice inside of you telling to take a risk and do that thing regardless what everyone might be saying or thinking.

This podcast or a business idea, a YouTube channel or a book club. Your own Facebook group, a chess club, game board nights. Maybe you want to approach someone that you really admire and would like to learn from that person. You would love for them to mentor you. Maybe there is someone you would love to do a joint venture with or go after that promotion you have been dreaming about. Maybe you want to finish that degree that makes you feel that you are not good enough every single time you think about it.

Go after it not because you want to impress someone with titles like, doctor, author, professor, CEO, barrister or PhD student. Do it because it is something you really want to do. Just take that first step. You are going to feel amazing about yourself. And you know what? That's going to make you look so damn attractive and sexy.

There is nothing better that a lady going after her dreams. When you are in your element, when you go after what you want you can conquer anything. You are invincible and this shines through. People can see that and they want to be around someone like that. They want to rub shoulders with a bad ass lady like you.

Go after what you want and you will be able to attract that quality person. Then you can be a power couple. Finding someone that does not feel emasculated by your greatness but celebrates and cherishes it instead by feeling proud waking up next to a lady like you.

Exercise. *Queen's Goals*

Write down that one thing that you have been thinking about but have not had the courage, resources or time to do.

Write down your 30-day plan how taking baby steps you will do something towards it.

Start now. What can you do today to start?

_____

_____

_____

_____

_____

_____

_____

_____

Get a printout from my website for a smart goal setting technique. I made it just for you. WhyAmIStillSingleBook. com

4. Smart is Sexy

Have you ever been at a speed dating event? If you haven't you have to do it. It's a rather interesting experience. You go to a place where you meet a lot of single people that are complete strangers. You get a designated time to speak to them. They go from one table to another. At the end you have to tick a box next to their names saying whether you would like to go on a date, be friends or if it is just a big fat NO. Next day you find out if you got any matches.

I have been to three speed dating events. The first time I went purely for research reasons and I met a cute guy. Brazilian, tall. We had an amazing date. Then he said there was no attraction from his side. I think it was more that he did not want to waste time with someone that did not want to have sex with him straight away. But that is absolutely fine. My friend thinks I am too smart for him and he just felt intimidated.

The other two times I went there and had zero matches. There was a guy with greasy hair and with no hair, a guy with nails of an eagle and a guy with nails that looked as if he went gardening and used his hands as gardening tools. There was a guy with big muscles and the guy that had a handshake that reminded me of a Disney princess.

The best part was when the conversations started. Something very interesting happened during two speed dating events I attended. And I know this is something a lot of ladies are concerned about. That is the reason you sometimes think you must dim your light in case someone thinks you are too much.

Firstly, I let men start the conversation as I could see they were quite nervous. And I have been blamed in the past for staring too much and for asking too many questions. What's wrong with that? I am only trying to look into your soul.

However, it got boring too soon and I had to take the lead to make my experience slightly better. I would just ask simple questions like 'why are you here, what kind of woman would you like to meet?' They gave me all kinds of questions.

Some of them just wanted someone they can go home to, chill, watch Netflix, eat pizza or have Indian take away after a long day at work. Sometimes to do things together. While I was listening, the little voice in my head was wondering how they are planning to maintain this relationship, how are they planning to make it interesting and exciting with Netflix and chill. But I did not challenge them.

There were two men during different speed dating events that left a big imprint in my memory. What was so special about them? When asked about their ideal partner, they said they would like to meet a lady who is lovely and beautiful, has a good heart, and is kind. The things that most of the guys mentioned. Mostly all of them stressing that looks are not that important, and that it's all about what's on the inside. Yeah, right.

Then I asked about their preferences in their potential partner's career. Does she have to be independent and accomplished? Does she have to be confident? Does she have to be ambitious and smart? The answer I got was this. 'I want her to be smart, but not too smart. I want her to be accomplished, but not too much. I don't want to feel that I am less than her. I want to feel like I'm the man in that relationship. I want to be in charge and I don't want her to make more money than I do.'

If you have ever met me, you would know that I am not very good at hiding my emotions and that I have one of the most expressive faces. But I tried to do my best to stay cool. I just kept asking him questions to see if he is going to correct himself. I thought it was interesting this guy admitted that he does not want her to be too much. And before your inner feminist wolf starts roaring, it's fine. That is his choice. Bless his socks.

I know that you have just finished reading the part of this book where I told you that going after your dreams is one of the sexiest things you can do. I still stand by it. You know a blogpost that's been on your mind for too long, but you think it's probably too honest and you just cannot reveal these things about yourself. That video you want to make, that business idea you have been sleeping on, but you think it is way too big for you. That promotion you would love to go for, but you keep doubting and thinking maybe it is too much and maybe you cannot do it. Go for it. You are a smart cookie. You can handle it.

Once you are in your element you will attract your kind of partner. Someone that celebrates your achievements and gets excited about your projects. Someone that lifts you up. You will also attract the kinds of people that support and celebrate you. Yes, some might feel intimidated by you, but these are not your kinds of people. It is just their personal preference. But there are people out there that can inspire you to reach the stars. Your job is not to forget that it is important to go for a walk and socialize while you are working on building that empire.

Always remember, smart is insanely sexy.

5. Your Network is Your Net Worth

If you are a business owner, an introvert, an entrepreneur, a high achiever, a mum, or a girl that just got into a new relationship or has broken up with someone or maybe you are just an awesome human being, there is something you have to remember. You might be isolating yourself. You need people to thrive.

Online businesses are taking over the world. Are you working from home? It sounds glamorous, but it can be lonely. On the other hand, you might be working in a big office where you interact with your team every single day. They can be a pain in the bum, but you have the advantage.

Guess what? You can use all these people whether they are single or married, unavailable or separated as your network. What do I mean by that?

Every single lady that you see at your workplace might have a single brother, a cousin or an amazing ex-boyfriend. If you share your lunch with a lady that kindly speaks about her husband, ask if he has any brothers or quality bachelor friends. And don't get me started about the number of single guys at your workplace. I'm not saying you have to come with an intention to find a husband every Monday morning or that you have to hook up at the Christmas party with at least one guy from your floor, just keep in mind that these people might have some single friends as well.

When you are at your workplace spend time getting to know people around you. Not only it can help you get a potential date, but you could have something fun to do during your breaks instead of scrolling on your phone. You might connect with some of your colleagues and form friendships. Also, that manager that always has her lunch by herself. Sit next to her. Tell her how great she is, find out about her dog. Make sure she remembers you when there is a spot for a promotion. You are a big girl and you know that at the workplace it is not how well you do your job, but it is about who knows about you.

I love people, but I tend to spend a lot of time by myself, because I do not know a lot of people that I really want to spend my time with. I have audited my friendships quite significantly in the last year and I have isolated myself, which was one of the reasons why my depression got out of hand. I am a social being, so are you. We need each other.

Spending time at the mental hospital and being surrounded by women that were supporting each other was amazing. Whether it was someone's first unescorted trip to the shop or three days with no self-harming signs, we all had something to celebrate about each other.

Also, that's the energy and the support I felt attending a retreat in Sicily. I felt invincible surrounded by the most amazing women. Women that were so encouraging and supportive. There is such a big misconception that women are always bitchy to each other and they are always competing. Women that dance with wolves want to support each other and see their sisters succeed. Find your tribe.

Loneliness could be one of the reasons you are craving that Mr Right. You think when you meet this person he will be able to be your shopping and gym buddy, your therapist, your best friend, the person you do your food shopping and laundry with. Someone you go out and enjoy tapas or a live performance of your favourite band with. One of the reasons so many relationships fail, is that you expect one person to be your everything. You need people in your life. Not just one person. Go out and find your tribe. It might not be easy, but you can do it. And once you have that amazing support system you will see what an amazing change it is to everything you do.

I am looking for my tribe. I have the Queen's Club where driven ladies like you connect online while sipping their favourite cup of tea. We discuss our goals and plans. We keep each other accountable. We support each other and celebrate each other's victories. If you would like to join go to my website WhyAmIStillSingleBook.com

6. Give Back

I matched with someone on Tinder. Yes, I am a big believer you can find love on Tinder. It is up to you how you use it. You will learn about genius secret Tinder techniques later in this book. But for now, back to my match.

We were just chatting. He wanted to see me on Sunday. I told him I couldn't, because I was volunteering at the local library. He was so impressed. He said, 'You sound like a really nice person, I like it'. I didn't think much of it. I volunteered at the library, because I wanted to have more experience working with children. I thought teaching was something I would like to do in the future.

This is a story about Ieva. A story about when she went to Cambodia. A story that tells about one of the proudest moments in her life.

In 2015 Ieva packed her backpack. She left everything behind and got herself a flight to Cambodia. She stayed in the middle of nowhere volunteering at the local school.

She slept on a bamboo mat sharing a little room and a mosquito net with other girls. They slept next to each other. When Ieva turned to her other side, the other girls turned too.

That was so comfortable compared to where most of the boys slept. Some of them had to sleep outdoors in hammocks tied up to coconut trees. Sounds romantic. But try sleeping like that for 12 months.

There was an outside bathroom. Ieva washed herself with buckets of rain water.

The school was overcrowded. It desperately needed an extension and a new bathroom, because there was only one for 50 students.

The funds could not be raised from students. Their families could hardly afford $25 monthly fee that covered their food and accommodation at school.

Ieva really wanted to do something about it. She saw how stressed out the school manager was. He said he needed $1000 to improve the school conditions. He had no idea where to get this kind of money.

Ieva created a charity to help raise the needed funds. With the help of her friends and family she was able to raise $1000. She was so proud and happy.

The moment she told the school manager that she had the funds was one of the most memorable in her life. No words could describe the amount of love and appreciation in his eyes. It filled her heart with love.

Giving back feels amazing. When you can see what a big difference an act of kindness can make, when you are helping someone without expecting anything back it empowers you. That energy is contagious, and people are drawn to it.

When I am coaching men I always ask them about the qualities they find attractive in a woman. One of the first things they mention is that they are looking for someone who has a good heart, is caring and loving. A lot of men would rather be with someone who is kind than someone with an incredible figure. Very often, even without understanding it, they look at you as a potential mother of their children. If you do things like volunteering and charity work, a lightbulb flashes in his head and suddenly he is drawn towards you, because you demonstrate the qualities he admires.

I believe it is important to give back and help others if you want to live a fulfilling life. However, no matter what you are doing make sure it is because you really want to do it and not just because you want to meet your potential partner. If you are thinking about some charity work, it is crucial that you take care of yourself first. You are the most important and you must fill up your cup first in order to help others.

wanderlust

noun

a strong desire to travel.
"a woman consumed by
wanderlust"

CHAPTER IV

Eat Pray Love

1. Woman Dancing With Wolves

Have you ever watched Eat Pray Love? I have a friend that says it's the cheesiest thing on this planet. I remember when it came out in 2010. I was watching and thinking how cool it was. I wished I could travel this much one day. Julia Roberts eating pizza, Julia Roberts exploring little alleys, Julia Roberts being in a country where no one spoke her language.

From a very early age I wouldn't care that much about what you own, but I would really envy you if you've been to amazing places. I remember during history classes I was learning about Christopher Columbus and his travels. I always thought about it as something out of this world.

Let's go back to 2015. I was scrolling on Facebook and finishing a late shift at a job where I didn't feel at all that I was dancing with wolves. I felt more like I was fighting with snakes inside of me. I came across this post about some random person that travels the world teaching English.

Fast forward 5 months later I had my own TEFL certificate and I was looking for a place to go and teach English. I found a place in Cambodia. Went there. Met the most amazing people. Learned incredible things about myself. I will always remember this trip as one of the proudest and heart-warming achievements of my life.

> *It was* Bon Om Touk, or the Cambodian Water Festival. *I went away to visit one of the sights. The most beautiful Otres in Sihanoukville. I was on a motorbike taxi with a complete stranger, who could not speak a word of English trying to get to a place I have never visited before.*
>
> *I remember sitting on that motorbike and feeling so free and fearless. Just like a woman that dances with wolves. I was so proud of myself that I did something that I really wanted. I was brave enough to go after my dreams. In that moment I felt that anything was possible.*
>
> *Then 10 minutes later he dropped me in a rather strange looking place and said that was my destination. For the next hour I was a woman that dances with unbearable heat. Walking with my backpack, looking for something—I was not even sure what. I managed to go to the wrong direction. It was so hot and I was so sweaty. But I remember looking at that clear blue sky getting lost in the most gorgeous ocean and feeling so grateful for being brave enough to go after what I wanted.*

You are your own goddess and you are here to have the most wonderful life. Do not let anyone tell you that there is something you cannot do. I will share my journey and what it meant for me to travel as a solo female traveller in Southeast Asia.

You might be someone that would love to travel, but you don't have anyone that wants to come with you. You might be even waiting until you find Mr Right. You think that once you find him you will do all those amazing things.

I used to think that way. I used to find it amazing when someone would say that they are travelling by themselves. But you know what? You just have to do it once and see how it feels. Go on a weekend getaway by yourself and see what you think. Then you can plan a bigger trip. Just be prepared to face the fact that solo travel is way more adventurous and exciting.

This chapter will be dedicated to you, the one with the tingling need to travel and explore the world. However, no matter what you are going after, whether you want to start a big charity organization or your own business, lose weight, get a mortgage, explore Siberia by train, start a podcast or anything else you can think of. No matter what that thing is remember that you are invincible. You are the Goddess. You can dance with wolves.

You don't need to run from wolves you can embrace them using all your beautiful feminine energy. You deserve to live fully. You know that feeling where you are sitting at your desk and wondering if this is all that life is? That feeling where you come back home after a long week at work and you feel lonely. You open a bottle of wine and you drink it by yourself. Then you have the whole packet of those cookies. Even though you promised yourself you'd only have one, because you are starting to go to the gym tomorrow.

You are buying that new dress. Sad, because you know you are not going to have anywhere to wear it, but it makes you feel better. At least you have the money to pay for it. You work so hard. But you do not spend enough time building and cherishing your relationships. You do not spend enough time doing what you love. When was the last time you did something not because you're after a great result or an amazing skill set, but just for fun?

Trust me, I know how easy it is to get caught up in the daily routine and how easy it is to forget and ask yourself, 'What do I really want? What am I here for?' You are here to be whoever you want to be. Don't let anyone dim your light. Have more fun in life.

I remember how I felt just before finding that Facebook post and going after my dream. Don't get me wrong, it wasn't all just roses and butterflies. I was scared. I was confused. But I did it anyway. There were challenges along the way. But that's the best part. Be your own kind of Goddess. Be that bad ass lady that looks at herself at the age of 80 and has no regrets. Because she lived to the fullest. You can too.

2. Solo Female Travel

What does solo female travel look like? What does solo female travel look like in South East Asia? I remember before going on my adventure I was Googling a couple of things. My flight was to Bangkok. When I googled Bangkok, I found a post saying Bangkok these days was a dangerous place to visit, because of the possible bomb attacks. I did not think much of it. I just thought whatever happens I am just going to embrace it. But it wasn't something I shared with my mum when she called me.

You know that feeling when you are starting to do something new and you are imagining how it is going to be? It was nothing like that. My most cherished memories involve the amount of love and kindness I have received from complete strangers, people that did not even speak the same language. I was loved so much. I was given meals and things by those that had so little, but they wanted to share. I was invited to their home. It was magical and I will never forget that.

There must be a disclaimer. I'm not an ordinary girl. I have this deep-rooted belief that everyone on this planet is kind, that everyone has good intentions. If they don't then it only means they are hurting inside, but deep down they are still loving and kind, because that is how we were born. I'm also a big believer that you see as you are. I know it sounds cheesy, but I truly believe that.

Before I share this, I think I must give you a warning. Please, do not try it yourself, because I do not know what might happen to you. I did it because it felt right. That's just how I roll.

Ieva was exploring Vietnam. She took a night bus to reach Hanoi. After a long 12 hour trip she got off the bus and the taxi driver insisted that she use his services. She did not want to do that. She wanted to walk instead and save a couple of dollars. But the taxi driver insisted that she go with him.

One of the people that travelled on the same bus was a Vietnamese guy she remembered from her previous hostel. He went to the driver to explain to him that Ieva did not want to go with him. The driver did not look happy. Ieva could not understand what the conversation was about, but the driver started shouting.

Suddenly, out of nowhere, Ieva saw a piece of brick flying towards the Vietnamese guy. The taxi driver was trying to hit him. Thankfully, the brick did not touch him. He said they should keep on walking and they did. Then he said that the taxi driver must be eating too much meat and sugar. Hence, the reason he was so angry.

Ieva dropped her bags at the hostel and continued hanging out with the Vietnamese guy and his female friend. She found out they were in Hanoi for a class reunion. They invited Ieva to join them. She had no plans. She was more than happy to join them.

First, they went to his friend's house where beautiful food was served. Ieva was invited to join them even though she had never seen these people before. They were lovely and extremely hospitable.

Then they went to their other friend's house where Ieva played video games and had a quick nap. The time for the fancy class reunion came. Ieva had a chance to see how wealthy Vietnamese people dine. A black Rolls Royce came to pick everyone up.

Ieva was introduced to everyone. She dined like a queen trying the foods she had never seen before and talking to people who organised events when Taylor Swift came around. Then they invited her to experience one of the most popular things in Vietnam, a karaoke. She went along. It was a great night.

Ieva was asked to stay at their house, but she already had a bed at the hostel. They were kind enough to give her a lift. Before dropping her off they invited her to join them the next day for some tea.

She did. Ieva told them about her travel plans and that she was going to the northern part of Vietnam. One of the ladies was concerned that Ieva did not have a bigger coat. She insisted that Ieva take her coat. Ieva refused, but she could see how much it meant for the lady that was offering it to her. She accepted the coat.

Ieva has a picture hanging in her room. It is a picture of her on the bridge during a very misty day. She is wearing that coat. It is a picture that reminds her to be kind. Always.

If I had a daughter and she told me about similar travel memories I do not think I would be very happy. I would wonder what if she got raped or kidnapped, chopped into small pieces and thrown into Mekong River. But none of that happened.

As I said, it is not something I would recommend doing as it is rather irresponsible and slightly risky hanging out with strangers, going to their house, having a nap there, getting in their car. That is everything your mum tells you not to do when you are growing up. But as I said, I am not an ordinary girl. For me it just felt right.

Now you know what kind of solo female traveller I am. Continue reading if this is something you would like to experience, but you think you have no funds or skills to do that. Let me show you that you can have the most amazing adventure even if you are single and broke.

3. Travel on a Budget

Sit down and with a piece of paper and your favourite diary and have a look at your recent spending transactions. Have a look at the last three months. Can you see where you are spending your money? Write down how much you spend on your skinny lattes, random tops you hardly ever wear, books you don't read, your gym membership, highlighters, moisturisers and serums, lash extensions and gel nails. Do you really need all that? How much did you get? This is the money you could be spending on travelling and exploring. £15 a day could take you places and fill your belly in exotic locations such as Vietnam, Cambodia, and Thailand.

You must have read or heard a story about someone fearless and incredibly adventurous who has travelled around the world with $10 in their pocket. You know that story I shared about very generous Vietnamese people? The truth is they did not let me pay for anything. I would have never accepted it from someone that had very little.

I appreciate kindness and I think it is so beautiful when a stranger wants to share dinner with you, but it is also important to contribute. If you do not come from an underdeveloped country, you must have enough money to pay for your food, accommodation, and transportation. Do not take advantage of people's hospitality.

When you go places where people do not have much, you will see that they are more likely to share, especially, with a lady who is travelling by herself. You might have a limited budget, and if you decide to go on the road, you will meet kind and giving local people who are more than happy to give you everything they have. I know someone who travelled across

Vietnam on a motorbike, had hardly any money, slept in a tent, and sometimes would crash in temples and stay with monks where he ate like a king. He has the most interesting stories to share. As much as it is nice to receive, you should always remember to give something back.

You have read about the importance of giving back in the previous part of my book. And you know that not only does it make you the most attractive wife material, but it lifts you up emotionally. It feels so good when you can share your gifts with others and when you can see what a big difference it can make.

If you want to improve someone's life, experience what it feels like to live around the locals, and travel on a budget, volunteering is one of the best options. There are organizations and businesses that are looking for people from all over world to come and volunteer to teach English, work at a farm or a bar, teach yoga and dance or volunteer at an orphanage. No matter what skills you have, no matter what your age or your education is, there is someone out there who would love to have you on board. It can be something as short as two weeks or a commitment for the whole year.

All you would need to do is pay for your flight. Once you are there, most places pay for your food and accommodation, and some might even give you pocket money. If they are really struggling, they might ask you for a small daily contribution to cover the expenses; for instance, $4 per day. There are volunteering programs out there that charge you thousands to be part of. It is up to you whether you want to spend your money towards a cause like that.

Before going anywhere, you should research the business

or the organization you will be staying at. You want to make sure it falls in line with your beliefs. You want to give your time for the cause you are passionate about, and you also want to make sure you have as much fun as possible. There are amazing opportunities all around the world. To find out more about how you can travel on a budget and volunteer abroad, download *Wanderlust,* a travel sheet with a list of organisations and websites you can contact today to plan your trip. Go to WhyAmIStillSingleBook.com

There are just so many books one girl can read and courses she can attend. There are just so many pairs of shoes she can wear. There are just so many planners she can have. Ditch all the unnecessary stuff, start budgeting more or even better, find ways to make money while you are travelling. Keep reading if it is something you would like to do. I have some ideas for you.

If you have never travelled alone, it might sound quite overwhelming. It's OK to feel that way. You are trying something new. Go for it. Stop scrolling and admiring Instagram girls travelling the world, bathing with elephants, playing with geckos and sipping fresh coconut juice wishing it was you. Do it yourself. If you get stuck in a foreign country and have no idea what to do contact me, I will help you. I promise.

4. Nomad Life

Is it just me or do you hear this word 'nomad' everywhere you go? The glamorous laptop life where you just work 2 hours a day while sipping your mojito and watching the blue skies, getting lost in the ocean. The get rich quick plans where you do not do much, but the money just keeps coming into your bank account. If you are not thrilled about volunteering and struggle to save up but cannot get the travel bug out of your system, there is another option for you: the nomad life.

If you are doing any kind of work where you are stuck staring at the screen all day long, you could be doing it remotely. Depending on your company's policy and the model of the business, your boss might be able to tailor your position to meet your needs. It depends if you are more than just a code at your workplace.

You could start with something such as Tim Ferris suggests in his book *The 4-hour Workweek.*[7] Start asking to work two days a week from home instead of coming into the office, showing your boss that you can increase your productivity and deliver better results. After a trial period, you could discuss something like going away for a week and still working on the projects that you are responsible for.

As long as you are able to show how the business can benefit from slightly changing the way you work, it could work out perfectly. If you don't ask, you won't get it. It is always worth trying. Remember when I was talking about your boss lady mindset and what Mel Robbins says when it comes to developing more confidence in the workplace. If you have no idea what I am talking about go back to *Chapter II.*

You can also quit your current job and get a new one. A lot of companies are looking to save and are more than happy

7 Tim Ferris, 2007, The 4-Hour Workweek: Escape the 9-5, Live Anywhere and Join the New Rich, Vermilion

to employ someone who won't rely on their workspace, national insurance, and training resources. For example, you are a digital marketer and you see a job advertisement online saying they are hiring for £30.000 a year. You contact them and tell them you can do this job remotely, agreeing to do the same job for 30% less than what they are offering. You could pack your bag and travel somewhere beautiful and sunny.

Imagine spending a month in Italy, then flying to France and Spain. There are places in Spain where you could rent a very simple accommodation for €200 a month. When you have enough of Europe you go somewhere else. You have so many skills that you could start monetizing. Are you good at writing a copy? Can you edit a video? Can you make a logo or maybe you are amazing with Photoshop? Are you an accountant or someone that could become a travel, lifestyle or home decor blogger?

You can always be someone's virtual assistant. As a virtual assistant you would be doing things like booking hotels, doing administrative tasks, contacting clients, chasing invoices and finding the best places to eat in town. There are thousands of small and big business owners who are looking for a remote staff. Get the *Wanderlust* travel sheet from my page to find all the relevant information about the best websites to look for remote work opportunities. Go to WhyAmIStillSingleBook.com

The possibilities are endless. All you need to do is to go for it. Just take that first step. Now. Stop reading this book and do it NOW. It is scary, but once you do it you will be wondering why it took you so long to start. Just like with everything with life.

Travelling is the best thing you can gift yourself. Once you start travelling the world, the way you see your surroundings changes. You also find a different side to yourself. The idea of getting married to a high school sweetheart sounds lovely, but you have the chance to be a woman that dances with wolves all over the world. Grab it while you can. And who knows. Maybe you will grab your very own Mowgli along the way.

Exercise. *The Goddess Super Powers.*

Write down all the skills you have. Everything you can think of. From bar work to doing spreadsheets.

_____

_____

_____

_____

_____

_____

_____

Now look at your list and highlight what you could do and make money while travelling the world.

Now you cannot say that the lack of funds is the reason you are not going on that big travel adventure. You are most welcome.

5. Expat Life

This is something you should never tell your mum, your girlfriends, your cat, your loved ones, your best friend. Sometimes when you go to foreign lands they do not feel foreign at all. Have you ever had that feeling?

You are visiting a place for the very first time, but it does not feel foreign at all. You just feel like it is your home. You love everything about it and you feel more alive. You feel so in tune with the surroundings. No matter what you do, you are flowing with so much ease. There is no resistance and things just work out so well.

The next thing you know, sights, scents, alleys and flavours that used to be foreign, suddenly become so familiar and so close to your heart. You don't want to part with them. You want to stay there. This is something that you should not tell your loved ones and your cat before going on that big trip. They are not going to be happy. Trust me.

What sometimes happens when visiting unknown lands is that you find that sense of belonging. That very special feeling you have been looking for a long time. Some girls move to unknown lands because they fall in love with a boy. While others move to unknown lands because they fall in love with the place, its people, food and culture.

It is a luxury. You might have a lot of commitments in your home country and you might think that moving to another country is impossible and absolutely insane. However, even if you have a car and a mortgage, a secure job and a handful of people that adore you to death, you could still become a woman that dances with wolves to the tunes unknown to her.

I want to tell you a story about a very special Girl. Her name is Greta. She is my youngest sister.

The first time Greta came to Vietnam was when she was visiting me during my 9 month backpacking trip. We were travelling for a while. Greta fell in love with Vietnam.

Greta wanted to live there. She came back to the UK, continued with the waitressing job she hated while doing her TOEFL course. She completed the course. Quit her job and went to Vietnam.

She got a job at one of the schools in Ho Chi Minh City straight away. She also got herself a handsome boyfriend. Later she got a cat. She broke up with her boyfriend. Now it was just her and her cat Noodle.

That's when she started doing something she has been passionate about for years. She started making cakes. She would work full time and then would hustle on the side.

Fast forward. It has been less than 12 months she has been making cakes in Vietnam and she is opening her own little cake shop. Yes, she has been working extremely hard to get there, but I am so happy for her. Proud big sister moment.

This could be you. No matter what your dream is you can make it happen.

Just like in any relationship, whether it's a relationship with a new country, a new hobby, a new man or a new relationship with yourself. When you go on a journey you never know where it will take you no matter how many entries you make in your perfectly organized bullet journal.

However, the best part is that when you decide to go somewhere you never come back the same. Whether you are a traveller, an immigrant or an expat, you will learn new things about yourself and the world. Nothing will ever be the same. For me this is the magic of travelling.

If you need support planning your big adventure get my *Wanderlust* travel sheet. Go to WhyAmIStillSingleBook. com

6. Dance in Your Own City

Don't you just love that feeling when you are at a place where no one knows you? You are so free. Sometimes you do not even need a cocktail to dance. You feel more relaxed when talking to people. You are a bit more fun and so much more chill. You are adventurous and curious about your surroundings.

When you are in a foreign country you can be the real you. No one is judging you. At least not people you care much about, because you know you will never see them again. Have you ever had a holiday romance? If you haven't, it's something you should try. Not that you can plan occurrences of this kind. When you are open to it, then the universe works its magic. Who says you can't be Julia Roberts in *Eat Pray Love*?

I had a client who was struggling to find a partner. Single for at least 5 years. A beautiful, smart and ambitious

project manager. Then she went on a business trip. She met an amazing guy. They clicked straight away. They drank wine. They laughed together. They stayed up till 4 in the morning just talking about life. The next day it was time to say goodbye. That was the last time she saw him. She did not use any initiative to let him know she would like to see him again.

When I asked her what made that night so special, she thought about it for a long time. She thought it was because he was so open and interesting, attentive and fun. Then she realised that the magic happened because she let her guard down. She allowed herself to have fun. She just stayed in the moment without trying to impress him. She did not have to waste any time wondering if he could be the one. Is he someone she could have a mortgage and babies, a dog and a cat with? Would her friends approve of him? She was in a foreign country and she knew she would never see him again. She just let herself enjoy that beautiful night staying in the moment.

You do not need to travel to another part of the world to have more fun. You can do it where you are, and you can even meet people in your local city. I know. What a shocker. It all comes down to how proactive you are. And when you are looking for those places to go remember your *Queen's Wishlist*. Where would your desirable partner hang out? If you have no idea what I am talking about go back to the very first chapter of this book.

You are a very beautiful but odd creature. You are a creature of habit. There are so many places around you that you have never visited. You keep going to the same coffee place. It is familiar. To experience something different you have to place yourself out of your usual surroundings. That's why travelling works so well. That's why you're more likely to have a fling during your holiday in Greece than staying at home and binge-watching YouTube videos.

So how can you dance with wolves in your own city? Explore your hometown as if it was a foreign land. Look at all the tourists having so much fun in your city, going to all the amazing places. They see your hometown from a different perspective. Tourists in your city look at everything with eyes full of excitement. There are a lot of gems around, you just need to start paying more attention. Think about all the new bars and restaurants that have opened in the last couple of years, but you end up going to the same one.

Have you ever been on a travelling website looking up 10 things to do in your city? What if you did and planned the most unforgettable day with someone special to you for some bonding time. When was the last time you went dancing? Do fun things.

Whether you decide to have a weekend getaway, or you are just taking a day to experience your hometown in a different way, you will notice a shift in yourself. Every time you do something new you discover new things about yourself. Whether it's trying a new dish, listening to an unheard song or looking at a beautiful painting that you have never seen before. You grow. Each experience gives you new petals. The more petals you have the more colourful your life becomes.

Exercise. *Rediscover Your Kingdom.*

Find out about the local events in your area. Find something that you find interesting.

Highlight that in your diary. Make sure you do not miss it. Wear something other than black.

If you are getting bored while you are on a date, just ask better questions. This person sitting next to you might not be the love of your life, but you can still have an amazing conversation.

CHAPTER V

Tinderella Diaries

1. Easy on the Filters

Let's talk all things online dating. If you are one of the biggest pessimists on this planet when it comes to online dating let me tell you that I have met some amazing guys on Tinder. With a couple of them I was even able to form long-term relationships. One at a time, obviously. Behave yourself. Will you please take off your online dating hater's hat and just be open-minded? You are about to learn some new tricks. But first things first.

Has it ever happened to you that you match with someone on an online dating site or maybe you've just been chatting on Facebook or Instagram, you are so excited to meet that person, but the reality is far from your expectations. He looks completely different compared to his pictures. Why why why?

He forgot to tell that he's gone bald in the last 5 years. He forgot to tell you he has put on a considerable amount of weight. In his pictures he is showing off a six pack. But here he is in his glory. And you know what the saddest thing about it is? You have spent all that time chatting to him. You have spent all this time imagining how everything will be and then you see him. He looks completely different from what you imagined him to be.

Suddenly, all those lovely nights spent chatting and sharing stories mean nothing. And no, you don't want to have babies with him. And you have to reschedule that wedding dress fitting. And you might as well go to Italy by yourself. I am slightly exaggerating, but I know that sometimes it's not that far from the reality. I have been there.

Ok, real talk time. You, lovely lady, you are so good at using all the filters. You might not know how to use Photoshop, but you are an expert at using all the other picture enhancing apps. You can make your thighs smaller. You can jut your chin forward. You can make your eyes look bigger. You know how to make your skin smoother. Well, that's just preschool business. Everyone knows how to do that.

The problem that I have noticed with men and online dating is that they put pictures that are not recent. Their pictures do not reflect their current reality. He's in his 30s, but that graduation party picture just looks too good to be replaced. Ladies are sneaky in a different way.

You know your best angle, you make your face look different with all that make up and then you top it up with a filter. That's one of the reasons men ask you to send a full body picture, because they want to see you. If you are a big girl and you are trying to put yourself as a smaller girl on Tinder, you are missing out on so much. What about those guys out there, who only love curvy girls? Embrace who you are, my dear Goddess. There is nothing more attractive than a woman who owns her body. A woman who owns who she is.

I'm not saying you have to put pictures where you show your face first thing in the morning, but don't overdo it with your make up, fancy apps and misleading angles. You want him to be able to recognise you when he sees you. I am not going to give you a lecture how I don't think you need full face make up every day to be beautiful, because you are beautiful as you are. But that's just me. I find women extremely beautiful. How your body moves, how you brush your hair, your voice. You are a woman meant to dance with wolves, not the woman to hide her shiny eyes under those fake eyelashes. Ok, I am done. I might have a title for my third book. *What Happens When You Stop Wearing Make Up.* Would you like to pre-order?

If you show who you are, and he does not swipe right you are lucky. You have just saved so much time, energy and effort. It just shows he is not the right match for you. I will talk about resilience and dating later in my book. For now, please, create that online dating profile if you are single. Do you want a fancier version of Tinder? Get swiping on Bumble.

Contact me for an online dating profile audit. I can look at your pictures and tell you straight away what that thing is that keeps attracting all the F boys. Go to WhyAmIStill SingleBook.com

2. Ask For What You Want

Whether you are a newbie or someone who has too much experience in online dating and finds it frustrating, there are certain things you can start doing now to make your swiping experience more enjoyable.

Let me guess? You like to read their bios. When I was writing my book for men *How To Get Laid Now* I went on Tinder to do some research work. I put men on Tinder to 10 different categories based on what they wrote in their bios. Let me share a handful.

1. A man of a few words. A man that cannot be bothered to fill up the bio or the one who is straight to the point showing off the strongest assets.

    Adam, 40. I have a 6-inch tongue and I can breathe through my ears.

2. A nice guy. An honest, loving, and caring guy. A man that is not afraid of his romantic side. These guys can be shy to start with, but it gets better once they feel more comfortable.

    Dan, 37. Genuine, funny, honest guy. Thoughtful, intuitive, and kind. Former A&E nurse, expedition medic & aid worker, now works in public health. Life is for living.

3. A funny guy. This is one of my personal favourites. Who doesn't like a good laugh? They usually have entertaining pictures as well.

    Craig, 27. I'm the kind of chivalrous bastard that holds a door open for an awkward amount of time. Honestly just want someone to tag in funny memes.

4. A kinky man. A man who is looking for certain things to satisfy his sexual desires. Very often it is a partner for a threesome. Most of the time,

a kinky man has rather descriptive bios and pictures.

Lord, 26. Hey, I'm single switch guy, very interested in exploring my submissive side. I'd love to meet an intelligent, open-minded girl that wants to explore kinks or her dominant side. Currently into face sitting + eating, pegging/strap-on play, tease & denial, and curious about many more. If I met a confident/bossy girl, then I have a 'try anything once or twice' kinda attitude really, ha-ha.

5. An angry man. Someone who is hurt, hates all women, thinks they are fake liars, and just cannot stand the world in general.

Nathan, 24. Do whatever the fuck you wanna do.

I have noticed there are a lot of guys who send rather strong negative vibes. They clearly state in their bios they hate animal filters, children, cats or gold diggers. Some express their love towards weekends away and gardening.

The truth is men will hardly ever read that beautiful description you got crafted on your profile. However, there will be some who will read it. You have to be smart and strategic about it.

Go back to your *Queen's Wishlist* that you created when I asked you to get more specific about the person that you would like to meet. Go back to that list that makes you excited, the one you read every other day before going to sleep. If you have no idea what I am talking about go back to *Chapter I.*

What could you include in your bio description that

would bring you closer to that person you would love to meet? There are guys out there who do their homework. The picky or more sensible swipers. They read your bio before deciding if you could be that special girl.

Add only what you want to attract. If you are not looking for one-night stands there's no need to say 'no hook-up's', because all he registers is 'hook-up's'. If you don't like liars and cheaters, there's no need to add that. It makes you sound that you are still recovering from your previous relationship. Be positive and fun in your bio. You attract who you are.

Some ideas what you could add to make it fun.

If you have seen Funny Games you stand a chance to get a coffee with me.

Why is this a good line? You tell about a film that you like. It's relatable if he knows what you are talking about. You sound cheeky and assertive.

You sound hot.
Three truths about me. Guess which one is a lie.
I swam with sharks.
I have two nipples.
I skinny dipped in Bali.

Why is it a great bio description? It is a game. It shows you are fun. You add some innocent nudity. He loves guessing. He wants to find out more about you. He is more likely to start a conversation with something other than just 'hi'.

Be creative when writing your bio. Also, make sure that your pictures tell a story. There is not much he can ask you about if there are only selfies of you. Show more of who you are. Let your pictures tell a story even if you don't look perfect in them. Have fun. I know it can be frustrating sometimes and you feel that you are wasting so much time and it isn't going anywhere. I will talk later how resilience is important when dating. But for now, just have some fun.

Contact me for an online dating profile audit. I can look at your bio and your pictures and tell you what you can do to attract a better quality man if you go to WhyAmIStill SingleBook.com

3. Make The First Move

Tell me if I am wrong, but I am convinced that men hardly ever approach women. Even if you are extremely beautiful and you look like a model, with your perfect hair and perfect nails. Your very perfect-looking foundation rocking that no make-up look. Your highlighter is on point. And don't even get me started on your style. You look amazing. Now whether you meet this description or not, I can guarantee you hardly ever get approached by men.

The ones that approach you are either the ones you don't want to talk to or they are so full of themselves and out of sorts that you just feel uncomfortable.

This is something I ask my male clients all the time. In fact, if I have a chance I try to ask this question of most men that cross my path. Why don't you approach women? The answers I get go from the ones where they say they do approach women, but when I ask for a specific example they cannot think of one. Others admit they never approach women concerned they might be not single or that they're out of their league or they don't want ladies to think they are harassing them. But most of them have the biggest fear of rejection.

Don't you think it is fascinating that a man can be a successful businessman, a public speaker earning 6 figures and teaching people how to live their best life, but he feels uncomfortable approaching a woman? He prefers to stay passive and just watch you. Even if you look at him or give him a little smile he is not 100% sure. He thinks you might be looking at the rich one, or the muscled one. He thinks it must be the tall guy you have your eyes on or that guy behind him. He needs to be sure it is safe to approach you. He is looking for your reassurance. His lack of self-confidence tells him it's just a coincidence, or that you're just being polite, but you don't really want to be approached. Do you think I am exaggerating? Sadly, not.

And that is the reason, my lovely Goddess, why I want you to be more proactive. Make the first move. You are a woman of high value. If you see someone that you fancy make sure he knows about it. Keep his gaze for a few seconds, give more than one subtle smile. That is enough for him to know it is safe to approach you. It's also ok for you to say 'hi' first.

Walk up to him. Have some fun. Make the first move. What's the worst that could happen?

The same rules apply to online dating. Be more in charge. You keep swiping and then you get a notification on your screen saying there's no one else available. You have run out of men. But I can guarantee you have so many matches that you have never spoken to.

What's the point of swiping if you never talk to anyone? Yes, some of your matches just wanted to see if they've still got it and how many matches they can get. They are only doing it for fun or they're trying to find out if their girl is on Tinder, because his mate said she was. Then he thought 'I might as well do some swiping since I am here'.

However, some guys are there because they would really like to meet you. Be the first one to make that move. Look at his profile and his pictures. See if you have something in common. But to be honest, none of that is necessary. Please, do not send him your life story that takes the whole paragraph. That is a bit too much. You are a woman. He will be more than happy just to get that message from you where you say nothing else, other than 'hi'. I am not a big fan of that and I think you can do better than that. But some dating gurus say you should not be investing too much. I don't think that asking about his favourite pizza topping would be a deal breaker.

Make a promise to yourself.

You are going to be more proactive and you are going to make the first move. It does not mean you are desperate. It just shows that you see something you like, and you are going for it. That's what women of high value do. You don't wait around watching your life and hoping that one day something will happen. You create these opportunities. And you have lots of fun doing it.

4. Call Him

You have matched on Tinder. You have been messaging each other back and forth for the last week. He even has your number. Everything is going well. He does not sound creepy, you seem to have a lot in common, you like his jokes and he hasn't even asked for nudes. It sounds promising.

Have you ever met a guy that was so laid back and so funny in his texts, but when you met him something was just not right? Firstly, you thought he might just be nervous, and you were waiting to see what happens next. How come you had such a good vibe messaging, but you didn't like him when you met him. I might have a solution for you.

How does it feel when he calls you? Doesn't happen that often these days. It's all about messaging. Don't you think that hearing that deep masculine voice can sometimes be exciting? Even receiving a voice message is so much more fun than just a text. I feel that the voice can tell a lot about the person. You can even feel when someone is smiling just by listening to their voice.

I want you to have a lot of fun dating. In order to do that you have to know certain things. I will cover a few more of those later, but for now remember this. Hearing his voice could be that factor helping you to decide whether you want to meet him.

His accent, his tone, his intonation. The way he articulates himself tells so much about him. I am from Lithuania and when I speak English you can hear my accent. Men love it. I remember when I used to work at the call centre I would hear all the time from male customers how much they loved my accent. However, there were occasions when I did not hear again from a couple of guys when I told them I was from Lithuania. Oh dear . . .

Also, if you meet online there is always that factor of awkwardness meeting for the first time. However, it feels different if you had a chance to speak with that person on the phone. He sounds more familiar. You also feel more relaxed and more comfortable around that person. You might be concerned about your safety while meeting strange men. Hearing that person's voice makes you feel more at ease.

But don't get me wrong. I'm not saying that a man who calls you before meeting you cannot be a rapist or a serial killer. Just making sure you understand this as I don't want someone coming after me and saying I am giving this kind of advice. Please don't shoot me.

How do you get him to call you? By asking. Just like everything in life. You cannot have something if you don't ask for it. And you know what's even better? You could call him yourself. Ask for his number and ask if it is OK if you call him.

If it's 10PM and he tells you he cannot answer his phone, but he just spent an hour messaging you I would think something fishy is going on. I think it is a very useful tool to find out if he is naughty or nice. He might be with his mates, which he would tell you about. He would also ask you if he can call you later. However, it is also possible he is with his girlfriend, wife, or partner. I am not going to get all worked up about it, but these things do happen.

Let's say he is ok with you calling him. Do it. Why not spend 10 minutes or so just chatting and seeing what he is up to. It's fun. First giggles, first awkward silences. Or you might have so much to talk about that you will spend hours on the phone.

If you are feeling brave enough, you could even initiate a FaceTime. You don't have to get ready for that or wear perfect make up. That hoodie you are wearing is perfectly fine.

Texting can be fun, but some texts can be misinterpreted just because you don't know that person. Also, some people are the worst at expressing themselves through text. I was once seeing this guy, who was flirty and fun in person, but sounded so grumpy when texting. It took me some time to get it.

Don't waste your time texting for weeks, creating happily ever after in your head, then meeting that person and feeling that you have nothing in common, wondering why your energies don't blend. Call him. He will be surprised. He will see you as a confident woman who uses her own initiative. It is hot Trust me. If you start talking to him on the phone and you feel you do not fancy him at all be nice and polite. Never harsh. Always treat others the way you would like to be treated.

Continue reading. I am going to ask you to be even more proactive. I've got you covered. Don't you worry, beautiful Goddess.

5. Ask Him Out

Who's got the time to spend hours and hours messaging someone that you might never meet in person? Having a deep conversation, feeling a strong connection and then, finding out that this person is not available and was using your chats as a distraction from his wife and everyday life. Yes, I make online dating sound really promising.

Also, before I continue, I must make a disclaimer. Stay away from all possible dating sites if you are hurting. If you had your heart broken and it has not healed yet, online dating is not a place for you. If you are feeling incredibly lonely, low or even depressed, online dating is not a place for you. You need a friend or a therapist. There is nothing worse than looking for these kinds of distractions when you are hurting. That won't solve your problem. That will only mask the pain, which will come back later. I am saying it, because I have done it. It was not a good idea. Please, stay away from it and find ways to love yourself first.

Ok, now back to the fun stuff. You know by now that it's ok for you to initiate the conversation. It's even ok for you to call him. Guess what? It's also OK for you to ask him out. Yes, I am throwing some nuggets of wisdom out here. You better be highlighting them with all the markers you have. You will need them later.

How do you ask him out? By asking. It does not have to be a dinner date. In fact, always avoid a dinner date as your first date. Even if he is asking you out. You do not want to be sitting with him feeling awkward if there is not much you have in common and if there is zero chemistry. You have better things to do with your time. If you are a food digger, I bow down to you. But I do not approve. I do not think you should be using someone just to get a free meal. You are a smart lady. You can find other ways to have a nice dinner without having to share it with someone you do not fancy at all and have no plans of meeting again.

Your time is valuable. Instead of agreeing to have dinner, suggest grabbing some lunch together, a cup of coffee or a drink after work. You do not have to stay long. An hour is fine. If you feel comfortable around him and if you are having fun, you can always stay longer. But make plans for just an hour.

It's ok for you to initiate it. If he works in town, but he

cannot meet you for the next two weeks for a cup of coffee I would be slightly concerned, especially, if he is able to speak with you on the phone during office hours. Is he married? Has he got three nipples? These things would be going through my mind. You can thank me later. I am just here to save you a lot unnecessary headache. Trust me, I have seen it all. Except for three nipples.

Do you know what's another great thing about meeting after work or during your lunch hour? You do not have to go shopping looking for something new to wear. You can just wear your work things. If you work from home, make sure you get out of those sweat pants. Remember to wash your hair.

The ultimate **Tiderella's checklist**:

- Easy on the filters.
- Make sure your pictures tell a story.
- Fill up your bio following the *Queen's Wishlist*.
- Include things in your bio that you want to attract.
- Make your bio sound fun.
- Stop swiping. Start talking.
- Get his number.
- Don't text him. Call him.
- Ask him out to see if he's married and loved.

If you follow these steps you should be fine. Before you start, please, keep in mind the magic won't happen overnight. If it does I would love to be your bridesmaid.

Always remember no matter what you are doing have fun. Don't look at each interaction wondering what's going to happen next. But also keep in mind that you can be in charge and you can speed up the process. Whether it's your soul mate or not. Swipe responsibly and remember to enjoy the process.

6. Stay Resilient

Sometimes dating might feel daunting. Strangers, small talk, not knowing whether that person likes you or not. Just that feeling where you are coming back from another date and wondering if there is something wrong with you. It seems that everyone around you but you is able to find a partner. Next thing you know they are married and posting baby photos.

You are smart, beautiful, healthy and funny. You have a good job and a handful of people that really love you. You are always learning and trying to grow and develop yourself. You are ambitious, and your career is going well. Why are you able to do so well in all other areas of your life, but your love life is non-existent?

If you've ever felt this way, you're not alone. And it's ok. It's ok to feel defeated when you have been trying something for a long time and it just isn't working. What if you just made a couple of tweaks and suddenly you could get different results?

First, make sure you go back to the very first chapter

of this book *Why You Will Marry The Wrong Person*. You might be in a dating rut or in a vicious cycle and you cannot see your way out. Do all the exercises guiding you towards your healing.

Have you ever seen that picture where two men are digging looking for gold? They are working so hard. They have both been digging for years. Suddenly, one of them decides to stop. He's had enough. He thought he must have been digging the wrong hole, because he worked so hard and he couldn't find any gold. The picture shows that he was very close to his fortune and he would have reached it if he just put in a bit more work and patience. What did the other man do? He continued digging and he was rewarded with gold.

Looking for love could be considered hard work, but it could also be a lot of fun. The quality of your conversations depends on the quality of your questions. If you are getting bored while you're on a date, just ask better questions. This person sitting next to you might not be the love of your life, but you can still have an amazing conversation.

It's important that every time you meet someone new you set a clear intention for yourself. I am not talking about the intention where you are saying you are going to have three children, a five-bedroom house and a horse with this person. I want you to think what you would like to experience while spending your time together. Would you like to be present? Could you be a better listener? Could you listen without thinking what to say next? Try that and you will see how much more fun it is to meet new people when you just let yourself stay present. In that very moment.

Do not let your previous experiences discourage you. You are constantly changing and growing. You will do better, because you know better. And if you don't, you'll still create the most amazing memories. Those lessons will be taught to you over and over. The only difference is that the next time it will hit you just a little bit harder hoping you will finally learn. You are a smart, powerful beautiful Goddess. You've got this.

Exercise. *Letting Go.*

Sit down comfortably where you are not disturbed. Write down in a column, the names of people you have been in a romantic relationship with. Relationships that did not go as you expected. Relationships where you were hurt or even had your heart broken.

_____

_____

_____

_____

_____

_____

_____

_____

_____

Look at those names and next to them write down something positive that each of these relationships have taught you about yourself. Only include positive things. Take your time.

There might be some tears. That's ok. You are healing.

Take a moment to think about these people and all the things they have taught you.

Send them beautiful love vibes. Take a deep breath in and out.

You've got this.

You are important. Your dreams,
your aspirations, your goals.
It all matters.

Ieva K.

CHAPTER VI

Stop Chasing Unavailable Men

1. Waiting is Sexy

When I was in my teens and in my early twenties I would judge women that would engage themselves in casual sex thinking it was so inappropriate and just bad manners. I am sure it has something to with the way I was brought up. Then I became more grown up and more of someone that is able to form her own views. Also, someone that wanted to experience her sexual desires. I became more lenient to what I thought was wrong and right in relationships. Sometimes too lenient.

Have you ever been in a situation where you meet someone, and you really like him, but you do things against your book? He is charming and cute, sexy and so fine. You have sex on one of the first dates or maybe even on the very first one. Sex is good, so you continue seeing each other and then the next thing you know 18 months have passed and you are still with that person.

He isn't someone you would like to plan your future with,

but it's nice to have him around. You do things together. You have a plus one at your friend's wedding. You don't have to go out of your way looking for sex. It's just there when you want it. You kind of got used to him. But then you start getting all those doubts. Is he the person you would like to plan your future with? No. Did you know that the first time you met him? Yes. Why are you still with him?

First things first. No, you have not wasted your time. Every relationship teaches you lessons. You get to learn so much from the person you spend your time with: music, new dishes and films, books and dreams. And that is all beautiful. However, if you are looking to get married and you are with someone you know who does not want to get married ever, why are you still together?

How does having sex on the first date have anything to do with that? I'm not saying that if you want to get into a long-term serious relationship that sleeping together on the first date is something you should never do. Absolutely not. Unless that person loves the chase and all that. That's everyone's personal choice. And if you are a free spirit and your idea of a great life involves having as many lovers as possible that is up to you as well.

However, if you are someone who would love to have a long-term relationship and you would like to find someone you could plan your future with then waiting can be sexy. Hear me out on this.

Have you ever found yourself going from one person to another and you just feel that it is not going anywhere? You end up in relationships that were initially just based on the physical connection, because you wanted to have sex or just feel someone's skin next to yours. Later you wanted to make something out of it, but it would not work. The next thing you know you meet someone else and it's the same story. Why not try doing things differently?

Why not go back to basics and do it the very old-fashioned way? Let him know that you find him attractive and that you like him and that you would love to sleep with him. But you would rather take things slow.

I have been in situations where I would tell a man I would like to get to know him first and there were occasions when that made him want me even more, because of all the preconditioned hunting instincts. But there were cases when he disappeared. That saved me a lot of hassle. When this happens, you can just get on with your life.

You know that feeling when you go on Facebook checking when he's online, waiting for the WhatsApp blue ticks to appear when he reads your messages. Saves you time, because you don't have to be passing by the places that he might be hanging around, obsessing about the fact he is not responding to your texts, or that he always seems to have a cold or a family emergency.

Then next thing you know he completely disappears. No texts, no calls for two weeks. You tell yourself you are a smart, independent and beautiful woman and you deserve so much more than that, but the moment he reappears with a good story, you pretend nothing has ever happened. Especially if he says how much he has missed you.

Go back to Chapter I *Why You Will Marry The Wrong Person* and see if there is a pattern in your dating life. If you can spot it, then start doing things differently. Sometimes it just helps not having sex on the first date. What if you could wait the first three weeks or even longer? It could be something else that you are doing that keeps getting you the same results. It's time to get rid of those patterns.

Exercise. *Letting Go of the Ghosts*

Write down 3 things you did in your past relationship(s) at the very beginning that you would like to do differently this time.

1. _____

2. _____

3. _____

What kind or results you think you could achieve by eliminating these behaviours and replacing them with something that is healthier for you?

---

2. You are Important

This is a story about a girl, who neglected herself and who thought that her life should revolve around that someone special.

Kate is a 34 year-old dancer. She is a smart gorgeous, talented and creative woman. She is a beautiful soul inside and out. She has an amazing body and a smile to die for.

Since she was a teenager she always had a big dream. She was not sure what it was. She just wanted to fill that emptiness inside of her. She thought her life would be different if she had a boyfriend. When she graduated from school with the best grades in class she was happy, but she thought none of that mattered, because she did not have a boyfriend.

Her prayers were answered. She had a man when she was 23. Then something interesting happened. Kate neglected her studies and her friends, her work and her colleagues. She did not even care that much to see her family. Everything revolved around her boyfriend.

She did everything she could to be the best girlfriend in the world. She did not like the food he ate, but she learned to cook it. She stopped watching her favourite films and listening to her favourite music, because he was not a big fan of them. She changed the way she dressed and the way she did her hair for him. She did his laundry. He paid all the bills. She did all she could to please him and be the best girlfriend in the world.

That was not enough for him. He met someone else. Someone who was a better girlfriend than Kate could ever be. More beautiful, with a better smile. She was better at cooking and had a more sophisticated taste in music. Kate wasn't that surprised. She knew having a boyfriend was too good to be true. It was just not for her. She was not good enough.

Then he came back saying how he preferred her cooking and her hugs, her kisses and the way she folded his socks and rubbed his back. Kate was happy. She started believing she was enough.

A few months later he did the same again. This time he did not come back. Kate wasn't surprised. She knew from the very beginning that having the happily ever after was not for her.

She went back to doing what she knew the best. She worked hard. She got a degree. Years passed by. She never dared to open her heart for love again. She did not think she was enough.

Kate is only 34. She can learn how to be in a relationship where she is important.

Can you recognise a part of yourself in Kate? Have you ever put someone else's desires before yours? Have you loved someone more than you love yourself? Have you ever thought that you are not important?

Kate doesn't know how to love herself. She doesn't understand that she's the most important person on this planet. You cannot share love with someone if you do not love yourself first. Fold your socks first. Cook that meal for yourself. Don't neglect who you are pleasing someone else. You are the most important.

I am someone that loves to nurture people and I very often put others first. I am the eldest of three sisters and I would always wait for my turn to get something. This habit has followed me later in life. If I cook dinner and one piece of salmon looks better than the other, I would give that better piece to someone else. If there are two cupcakes on the table and I am sharing them with someone and that person asks me which one I prefer, I'd say I don't mind even if I do. I let them choose.

These are small examples; however, these habits often lead to something bigger. If you made plans and your date is forty-five minutes late, are you going to confront it or you are just going to play it cool, because you don't want him to say you are overreacting or that you're being dramatic?

When you are someone who never voices her opinion, and who always puts herself second, who is always thoughtful, but forgets her own wishes and desires, often you will attract the complete opposite. You will attract someone who does not care what your opinion is and even takes advantage of your beautiful heart. You will attract someone who will bully you or even abuse you. That's the reason you must look after yourself and make sure that you're not being used by someone who might be taking advantage of your thoughtfulness. Learn to put yourself first more often and don't take it for granted when someone you love is ignoring you. Watch what they do, not what they say.

You are important. Your dreams, your aspirations, your goals. It all matters.

I am not telling you to be a self-centred bitch that never takes into consideration what others want. However, if you are sticking around someone who visits you only when he wants, but always cancels when you plan something together, however, you never have the courage to confront it, because you think of too many reasons why it is acceptable. Why is his time more important than yours? Then deep down you wish you were around someone who was more present. Someone that makes you feel you are wanted.

Voicing your wishes is the first thing you can do. Every time you want something, and you do not voice it you let yourself believe that you are not important. Good news. There are ways to heal from it.

> **TIP**
>
> The next time you have to choose something, think what you would like to do the most. Don't wait for everyone to express their wishes. Say what you want. The more you do it, the better you will become at it.
>
> I am learning this every single day. It's a great skill to have for a high-quality driven woman like you. You are important. Never forget that.

Exercise. *Proud Queen.*

Write down 10 things you are proud to have done in the last 9 months. They could be anything. From learning to love your body to finally mastering your frizzy hair or learning to make Bolognese from scratch.

1. _____

2. _____

3. _____

4. _____

5. _____

6. _____

7. _____

8. _____

9. _____

10. _____

3. Get a Life

I did not write this book to tell you that you don't need to be in a relationship to be happy. I hope you are not a lady who thinks she will be seen as less smart, less ambitious, less driven, less intelligent if she says out loud she would like to be in a loving relationship. There's nothing wrong with that.

Your life is like a puzzle. It's made of so many different pieces. Your dreams, aspirations, your health, family and friends, your work and body, your diet and your mind. You have so many different pieces to yourself, so many different sides. And you keep evolving. You are growing and changing all the time.

I am not saying don't be in a relationship and spend time alone and rock that 'I'm my own kind of woman and I don't need anyone' life. However, dear Goddess, do not make finding that special someone your only goal in life.

This is a story about Aiva.

Getting married has always been one of Aiva's biggest dreams. She thought that once she settled down, got a house and a husband her depression would go away. She felt empty.

She met someone at her workplace. They got on well. They did not spend much time together, but she felt happy. Her depression would sometimes creep back. She distracted herself with her love life.

He proposed. They moved in together. Aiva spent 12 months planning her wedding. Finally, she was going to have what she always wanted. She planned every detail. She had the most perfect wedding day.

However, two weeks later she could not recognise herself. Nothing brought her joy. Her husband was always spending time at the office. She did not have many friends left, because after meeting her future husband she only concentrated on him. She had nothing she could look forward to. Aiva felt she had no life.

Her depression got out of hand. Her husband could not understand what was happening. He spent even more time at the office. He started going on business trips. Too many of them. Aiva was crying for help, but all he could see was a spoilt miserable little girl.

Aiva started seeing a therapist. She learned a lot of things about herself. The day she met her husband he made it very clear he would never be available for her in the way she wanted. But Aiva chose to ignore it. All she wanted was to get married.

What can you learn from Aiva?

Don't you think it is interesting that when you were growing up you would hear how to be a good wife, but not how to be a great friend? You have been taught how to do house chores, but not how to voice your opinion or love yourself. Well, maybe it is just my Eastern European upbringing.

However, if you invest into yourself, your growth, your gifts, your aspirations and dreams you'll be able to have the most amazing life. The better you know yourself the more you'll understand your worth. When you know your worth, you do not surround yourself with people that do not appreciate you. Instead, you are around those that celebrate you. Am I the only one suddenly thinking about Alicia Keys and her song *A Woman's Worth*?

Me: drop everything and going on YouTube to listen to *A Woman's Worth*. The lyrics suddenly had a completely different meaning than they did back in 2001 when the song came out. Yes, that long ago. I have checked.

Before you obsess over someone not messaging you back find out answers to these questions.

When do you feel loved?
How do you deal with rejection?
What is your love language?
What is your biggest childhood trauma?
When do you feel the happiest?

Find things in life that you feel passionate and obsessed about. Go after what you want. Sign up for that class, learn that language, go for that job interview, get that promotion, work on that idea you have been sitting on for the last 5 years. Do things you love. Get a life instead of obsessing over someone who is clearly not investing in you.

Why do you even want to be in a relationship? Is it because all your friends on Facebook started posting pictures of baby number two and you are still dancing by yourself in your bedroom? Are your parents pushing you to be in a relationship? Do your parents even know you well or do they just know the version of you they want to see?

You are bombarded every day with advice telling you what is wrong with you and what you must fix about yourself. But if you're someone who does not like your job, you don't have any social life, you do not remember when the last time was you went out, and you feel uncomfortable every time someone asks you about the things you love doing and you cannot think of anything exciting. Well, girl. Get a life.

You can't be just waiting around hoping he messages you. Get busy living instead. Don't try to fix your life with a relationship. Fix your life first and let the relationship flourish there. You can't build a house on a crumbly base. You are a beautiful Goddess. You deserve to dance with wolves and not crawl after them.

4. 37 Things Queens Do

Please don't hide if you just finished reading the *Get a Life* part and you feel it all sounds great, but you just cannot help yourself. You know he's trouble, but he is just too good to resist. You know it isn't going anywhere, but you just want to try one more time, because the way he makes love to you is just too sweet to be missed. And you end up in that never-ending vicious cycle.

You saw him last week. You haven't heard from him since then. You can see he is online, but he isn't contacting you. I used to be someone that would never message first. I used to be that person that I would just wait till he messaged.

Things have changed. If I had a date and I enjoyed it, I am going to message him.

What if he isn't responding? Well, I haven't been in that situation recently. Things have changed, and I have not been attracting any unavailable men. I've learned from my previous mistakes. I know I could help you as well.

However, in the past I was so good at coming up with too many reasons why he was not texting me back. He's probably busy at work. Poor baby, he might have a flu. Maybe something happened to his dog. He might have had a death in the family. You know the game. It's ok. You don't have to hide. I've done it as well.

You're waiting for him to message you. You are waiting for him to come and see you. You are waiting for him to make your day better. You promised yourself you wouldn't message him, because you know he isn't good for you. But you just cannot help it. You crave him. You know he'll disappear again, but you are willing to risk it.

I don't want you to obsess over him. Do something fun instead. Take care of yourself. I present you an ultimate Queen's to do list. 37 things you can do instead of messaging him. I've been in those situations and I wish I'd had a list like this back then. It would have saved me so many headaches.

37 Things Queens Do

1. Meditate for 10 minutes.
2. Do yoga stretches.
3. Run a bubble bath.
4. Do a full body scrub.
5. Massage your hands and your cuticles with a lovely smelling cream.
6. Do your nails.
7. Listen to an upbeat playlist.
8. Got for a walk.
9. Scrub and massage your feet.

10. Learn how to do a headstand.

11. Journal.

12. Do your monthly goals list.

13. Watch something inspirational on YouTube.

14. Read a book.

15. Write down 10 things you like about yourself.

16. Call your friend.

17. Go to your favourite coffee place.

18. Call your mum.

19. Sort out your wardrobe.

20. Give unwanted items to the charity.

21. Cook a delicious meal.

22. Look up things happening around you. Go out.

23. Call your friend.

24. Visit a gallery/museum.

25. Write down 10 things you have achieved in the last 6 months that you are proud of.

26. Sign up for a cooking class.

27. Put on a face mask.

28. Put on a hair mask.

29. Have a nap.

30. Write a poem.

31. Call your friend and ask if they need help with anything.

32. Spend 5 minutes just sitting and brushing your hair.

33. Go on Instagram and leave 10 beautiful comments acknowledging people.

34. Do a food prep for the next 4 days.

35. Call someone you love and tell them they are amazing.

36. Write down 7 reasons why you are more important than that person that you can't wait to have a text back from.

37. Stand in front of the mirror and say out loud 7 reasons why you are more important than that person that you can't wait to have a text back from.

Try and see how it goes. I am not expecting you to do all 37 things from the list. Well, I have never met someone that hot. By the time you complete at least 3 things in no particular order you should feel much better about yourself.

I made this list for you not because you are childish, and you don't want to message him first. This is for you when you realise that what is going on between you and that person is probably not that healthy. This is for you when you realise you have a pattern of these unhealthy relationships and would rather invest your time and energy into something that radiates with more self-love and care.

A little secret. Would you like to know how I came up with this list? When I was at the mental hospital I had

Cognitive Behavioural Therapy sessions. I told my therapist I struggled with negative self-talk and anxiety. She gave me a list of things I could be doing to distract myself when I know one of those episodes is coming my way. I thought it was an amazing way to distract myself from other things that are not good for me. And here you are. I have added like twenty things to it. You are most welcome. No more F-boys.

If you need a tribe of ladies to keep you accountable make sure you join my *Queen's Club*. Go to WhyAmIStillSingle Book.com

5. Listen to Your Gut Feeling

One of the biggest lessons that I learnt when I went away to Southeast Asia, especially visiting some rural areas, was that people were more in tune with themselves. They were more peaceful. It seemed that they felt more. Even when I could not understand a single word said to me I could feel people just by looking at them, at their eyes and facial expressions. I felt more connected. We are so good at thinking in the Western world, but often we forget how to feel.

When you are at school and you are learning new things, you are told that thinking is more important than feeling. Very often feeling is placed in a box towards something that is considered as a sign of weakness. Meanwhile being a sharp thinker is always encouraged and celebrated. The masculine and feminine sides. I hope you are not neglecting either of those and making the most of your feminine gifts.

Whether you call it your inner voice, your intuition, your gut feeling or your inner wisdom, I'm sure you have experienced moments in your life where something stronger than your body was sending you a signal about a certain place, situation or a person.

Let's bring it to dating. You are meeting someone for the first time and this person seems interesting, charming, fun and not bad looking. But something does not feel right. You cannot quite put your finger on it, but you just have this funny feeling. Your body is telling you shouldn't follow up with this person, but you are so out of sync with it that you just choose to ignore it. Fast forward you are chasing him. He is ignoring you. Then he is coming back. 12 months later you find out he has a wife and a child he forgot to tell you about. This has happened to me. Real story.

I remember I was dating someone, and I would get this feeling of unease in my tummy when he would ask me questions about our future together. Also, when sleeping at his place I would struggle to sleep. I hardly ever have a problem falling asleep. But I did not understand what my body was trying to tell me. I couldn't tune into my intuition. The noise in my mind was overpowering it. I did not understand that something was not right.

Let me just mention that at that time the guy was nice and very available. I was trying to convince myself I loved him and wanted to be with him. It was the first time I was in a relationship with someone I did not have to chase after. However, no matter how nice he was my inner wisdom was rejecting him. If only I listened to that inner voice. I wouldn't have lost that deposit I put down for that big three-bedroom house. You have just witnessed a phenomenal example of my dark humour.

You, beautiful Goddess, are given this amazing feminine power for a reason. I mean your intuition, not the dark sense of humour. Don't neglect it when you experience it in a work or business situation, when you are about to sign a contract, take up a new project or let a new man into your life. If something does not feel right, it probably isn't.

How can you become more in tune with that special power?

Make sure you have your night/morning routine in place. Go back to Chapter II *You're The Goddess* to remind yourself how important it is to have one and what happened to me when I neglected myself. Your morning/night routine helps you to get in tune with yourself. You react less to all the external noise while being able to focus on what you want, what you feel, what you wish.

Meditation and yoga can also be helpful when tuning into your inner wisdom. It's something I do not do as regularly as I would like to. I am going to do better. I promise.

Mindfulness. Practice being in the moment. When you are eating avoid looking at the screen. When you are walking down the street take a moment to look around and enjoy your surroundings. Slow down as much as you can. When you are having sex do not think about your to-do list. Just have sex.

The more you practice these things the more you will notice that something is opening within you. The more you act on what feels right the more you will start experiencing magical things. When you listen to your gut feeling and move yourself from something that isn't good for you, you're attracting the very best for yourself at the same time. Your mind is capable of amazing things. When you learn to block the outside noise and tune into your inner wisdom nothing is off limits.

6. Free Yourself

I have a confession to make. I am very good at self-sabotaging. I'm very good at convincing myself that I don't want certain things in life or that they are unavailable for me. I have experience being in relationships where a man made it very clear that he did not want to have a future with me. He made it clear he was not available, but I chose to ignore it.

I even had occasions where I convinced myself I wasn't even the marrying kind. I told myself I was too busy building my empire. Too busy conquering the world. I neither have the time nor wish to have a husband, babies and a dog.

Disclaimer: I am still not 100% sure I want all that.

Everything is available for you. You can have a beautiful place to live. You can have that inappropriately big and furry dog. You can have a great career that you love. You can have a man that absolutely adores you.

I would be a liar if I said I have mastered all of it. I don't have that rock on my finger and I am not even sure I want that. However, one thing that I really know is that I was able to set myself free. I have managed to break that never-ending vicious cycle of unavailable men.

I still have some healing to do, because I still find the idea and the image of tall, dark, handsome and unavailable rather attractive. But there is massive progress. I acknowledge the situation. I assess it and I can walk away from it. I have stopped lying to myself. I have set myself free from unavailable men. Because I know I deserve better. I know I deserve to be loved.

No matter what you are going through you can change it. Even if you had your heart shattered into the smallest pieces and you think you will never be able to love again.

Or maybe you have never been in love and you feel there is something wrong with you. You can change it. It won't be easy. The change is uncomfortable. But think about all the new possibilities behind it.

I love how Deepak Chopra describes the law of detachment in his book *The Seven Spiritual Laws of Success*. It perfectly describes the journey you might be on.

> *'Relinquish your attachment to the known, step into the unknown, and you will step into the field of all possibilities. In your willingness to step into the unknown, you will have the wisdom of uncertainty factored in. This means that in every moment of your life, you will have excitement, adventure, mystery. You will experience the fun of life—the magic, the celebration, the exhilaration, and the exultation of your own spirit.*
>
> *Every day you can look for the excitement of what may occur in the field of all possibilities. When you experience uncertainty, you are on the right path—so don't give up. You don't need to have a complete rigid idea of what you'll be doing next week or next year, because if you have a very clear idea of what's going to happen, and you get rigidly attached to it, then you shut out a whole range of possibilities.*[8]

This journey is not going to be the smoothest one, but that's the beauty of it. You are going to gain so much

---

8 Deepak Chopra (1996), *The Seven Spiritual Laws of Success*, Bantam Press.

inner wisdom, peace and love. If you feel you need a tribe to make the transition less lonely get in touch with me at WhyAmIStillSingleBook.com

I can introduce you to a tribe of ladies that dance with wolves.

Continue reading to find out more about yourself and to learn to deal with challenges that Disney forgot to mention. For now, set yourself free from what you think it is unavailable for you.

Exercise. *Queen's Dreams*

Write down 10 bad-ass things you would love to do in the next 10 years.

1. _____

2. _____

3. _____

4. _____

5. _____

6. _____

7. _____

8. _____

9. _____

10. _____

It would be fun if you could post it on Instagram. You would inspire other girls to be more bad-ass.

Please, tag me @ieva.kamb or search me by my full name IEVA Kambarovaite in case I decide to change my IG name.

This is my list.

1. Skinny dipping in Bali.
2. My birthday party with the infinity pool.
3. A road trip on a motorbike. I am riding it.
4. Playing with 10 kittens at once.
5. Spending the night in one of those hanging tents in the sky.
6. Trekking in the Amazon.
7. Climbing Kilimanjaro.
8. Making tiramisu from scratch.
9. Driving a race car going over 100 m/h.
10. Getting a puppy.

It takes a one bad-ass high quality woman to admit when she is wrong or overreacting. It also takes a very brave one to walk away from someone who hurts her.

Ieva K.

CHAPTER VII

Tell Him What You Want

1. He's Not a Mind Reader

There is this very interesting idea that has come from Romantic era and is often demonstrated in Hollywood films and love stories. When you meet the right person, when you meet your soul mate, everything will be perfect. He will be able to read your mind without you even saying a word.

I don't buy it. The only people that can sometimes read my mind are my sisters. I end up buying the same clothes as my middle sister without even realising it. I do have quite an expressive face, so very often it is not that difficult to understand if I dislike something. However, I have learned the hard way that my lover is not the mind reader. If I want something I have to say it.

Indeed, it does happen when you spend a lot of time with someone you are able to finish each other's sentences. But I find it is easier done with women than men. I guess that's just the power of the feminine force and our ability to be so observant and intuitive.

One thing you have to understand is that a man thinks of you as the most complex being. The way your body moves and feels, the way you think and your unimaginably complex ability to multitask. He finds it amazing how you are always better at spotting when the milk is off, and you are the first one to spot he has been wearing that shirt for too long. He sees you as a never-ending mystery.

And don't get him even started on the things in the bedroom. The second he thinks he has figured out what makes you come you suddenly declare that you do not like that position at all. And that's the reason you have to be slightly more accommodating. He is not a mind reader. Tell him clearly what you want.

A rather simple example. You ask him to pick a take away. He asks to you tell him what you want. You say you are easy, but then you don't agree with any of his suggestions. He is not a mind reader. Just tell him what you want. Food can be a complicated matter. I get it.

When you start seeing someone new you have to teach him how you want to be treated. It is your responsibility. He doesn't know you. You have to tell him about your boundaries, what you accept and what you do not tolerate. No need to discuss that on the first dinner date or in front of his friends. Find the right place and the right time for it.

He had a different upbringing to yours. He might even be from a different country or have a different religion. He wasn't brought up the way you were. He had different experiences in life. It might be that this is not his first relationship. He doesn't know what he doesn't know. It is your responsibility to teach him.

I have been in so many situations feeling I was disrespected by a man. Later I realised I didn't set clear boundaries. It was my responsibility to teach him how I wanted to be treated. It was my responsibility to tell him I did not appreciate when I had to hide while driving in his neighbourhood. But I stayed quiet holding it all in. Then I started feeling bad about myself. Feeling that I did not matter.

I know you want that deep connection where you can feel it in your bones. You want him to get you. You want him to understand what you are thinking without even voicing it. But why not take that power into your hands. Instead of waiting for him to process it through his own filter, just tell him what you want. Whether it's in the kitchen or in the bedroom just tell him what you want.

This is where the success of 50 Shades of Grey comes from. Women are watching it thinking Mr Grey knows all the parts that have to be touched and kissed. The sad part is that most women took their partners to watch that film or handed their men books highlighting their favourite parts. These women hoped their partners would be able to understand that was something they wished their men could replicate in their very own bedrooms.

He does not understand your subtleness. You must be clear. Tell him what you want.

2. Know Your Love Language

You know he is not a mind reader, so you make a conscious decision to do your best by telling him what you want. But you have days where you yourself are not even so sure what you want. It might be even causing you a great deal of frustration if you are a control freak. Please, do not shoot me for this overgeneralisation, but a lot of us, ladies, are complete control freaks. Yes, I said it.

What if you knew exactly what he has to do to make you feel loved? What if you could explain to him in the simplest way when you feel the most appreciated and valued? What if you were able to give him a simple formula, which would help him understand how you operate? The truth is, if he loves you, the main thing he wants in this relationship is to make you happy and see you smile.

For this to happen you have to be highly self-aware. Yes, that same big word that seems to solve all the problems in the world but takes a lifetime to develop. It's ok that you feel confused looking at your best friend, who is the happiest when her hubby leaves love notes all over the house. It's ok if this does absolutely nothing for you.

I remember I was in my early teens and there was a Jennifer Lopez music video going around *Love Don't Cost a Thing*. The story goes like this. She's seeing someone super busy and rich. He buys her diamonds but does not have the time to spend with her. She gets upset and shows that love is not about that, because love don't cost a thing. I remember watching it and feeling so confused thinking how spoiled this lady was. She's got this man that buys her bling and she is still not happy. Well, now I know exactly what she meant.

Dr Gary Chapman, the author of the book *The Five Love Languages*[9], solves this big dilemma in a very simple way. He says there are five different ways in which we show and understand love, whether it is a romantic partner, your best friend, or a family member.

---

9   Gary Chapman (1995), *The Five Love Languages: How to Express Heartfelt Commitment to Your Mate*, Chicago, Moody Publishers.

Words of Affirmation: Expressing love by using words that include verbal compliments and words of appreciation. It could be expressed with simple statements like, "I love you," "You are so smart," or "You are so good at your job." If this is your love language, you react in a sensitive manner when criticised. Recognising it can help you to understand yourself or your loved one better.

Quality Time: The love language where you feel most loved when you get to spend quality time with another person. It cannot be just sitting and watching TV together; you have to do things like going for a walk, having a dinner, or talking where it is just two of you, and you can experience undivided attention. If your love language is quality time, you might get really annoyed when you are having a special night out and he is on the phone.

Receiving Gifts: Understanding love through unexpected gifts is not about the physical thing that you're getting, but it's the thought that is important. You feel loved and remembered, because someone took their time to express their love. It doesn't have to be anything big, just a small gesture. Do you remember that Jennifer Lopez video I was talking about? He clearly did not know her love language.

Acts of Service: Acts of service means you feel loved when someone does things for you. You feel loved when he does the dishes, makes you a cup of tea or rubs your feet. Sometimes it requires time, energy, planning, and some extra effort, but that's why you love it so much.

Physical touch: Holding hands, embracing, cuddling, and sexual intercourse are all ways of communicating emotional love to someone who understands love through a physical touch. If this is one of your love languages, you feel loved the most when he is holding your hand in public or gives you a little kiss.

I can't think of many things that could top the gift of being around someone who wants to learn with you. Someone who wants to learn about you without prejudging you, without thinking they know it all. Someone who is continually striving to improve the way you communicate with each other. It is an amazing gift that you can give to someone.

You can avoid so many misunderstandings if you know yourself well and you can guide others showing what makes you tick. They do not know you. It is your responsibility to get to know yourself and teach others how you want to be treated.

3. 37 Ways to Connect

More than anything you want that deep connection. The kind of connection where you stay up late talking about nothing, but also about what really matters. The connection where you pick up the phone to message him and you can see he's just messaged you. Then you get that great feeling in your tummy. You both are thinking about each other. Then you reach the point where you can finish each other's sentences. You feel you just know everything about that person.

The unknown keeps you on the edge at the beginning of your relationship. You want to avoid it, because the unknown is causing you a headache. Not knowing if he will call you, not knowing if he finds you attractive or whether you will see him ever again. However, later the very unknown is also what you crave.

Something interesting happens when you spend a certain

amount of time with that person. I have done it too many times and I am not proud of it. You assume. Indeed, you might know a lot of things. However, by assuming you miss a chance to know more.

I have something that will help you to connect and get to know your partner much better whether it is your 1st or 101st date. 37 questions to build a connection. 37 questions to help you connect with another human being at a level that you have not experienced before.

Go on a date or have a relaxed night at home. Sit next to each other and open your heart and your soul to the unknown. Don't interrupt each other. Allow the pauses. You will feel vulnerable. You will feel as if someone is looking into your soul. You will also feel the most beautiful connection. Enjoy.

37 Ways To Connect

1. How are you mad?

2. Would you like to be famous? In what way?

3. What are you most excited about in your life right now?

4. What would be a "perfect" day for you?

5. When did you last sing to yourself? To someone else?

6. If you were able to live to the age of 90 and retain either the mind or body of a 30-year-old for the last 60 years of your life, which would you want?

7. Would you rather lose your legs or your penis?

8. What's your biggest fear?

9. For what in your life do you feel most grateful?

10. If you could change anything about the way you were raised, what would it be?

11. Take four minutes and tell your date your life story in as much detail as possible.

12. If you could wake up tomorrow having gained any one quality or ability, what would it be?

13. Given the choice of anyone in the world, whom would you want as a dinner guest?

14. What is the greatest accomplishment of your life?

15. Is there something that you've dreamed of doing for a long time? Why haven't you done it?

16. What do you value most in a friendship?

17. What is your most treasured memory?

18. What is your most terrible memory?

19. If you knew that in one year you would die suddenly, what would you change in your life?

20. What roles do love and affection play in your life?

21. What are the three qualities you most admire in others?

22. How close and warm is your family?

12. How do you feel about your relationship with your mother?

13. Complete this sentence: "I wish I had someone with whom I could share . . . "

14. Do you believe in the concept of the one or a soul mate?

15. What's one of the most embarrassing moments in your life?

16. What do you wish you did more in your life?

17. When did you last cry in front of another person? By yourself?

18. What, if anything, is too serious to be joked about?

19. What's your definition of greatness?

20. What would you put on a billboard?

21. What is your legacy?

22. If you were to die today with no opportunity to communicate with anyone, what would you most regret not having told someone? Why haven't you told them yet?

23. What's your biggest fear?

23. Your house, containing everything you own, catches fire. After saving your loved ones and pets, what else would you save?

24. What would you do differently if you knew nobody would judge you?

25. Do you treat yourself with the love and respect you truly deserve?

26. Why do you get uncomfortable talking to people you don't know?

27. What is one thing you could start doing today to improve the quality of your life?

28. When was the last time you told yourself "I am enough"?

29. Who inspires you the most in this world?

30. If you were to give one piece of advice to a newborn child, what would it be?

31. Are you holding onto something you need to let go of?

32. What do you think about when you are alone?

33. What are you most passionate about?

34. Where do you think will you go after you die and what's going to happen to you?

35. Who are the people that believe in you?

36. What is one thing you love the most about yourself?

37. What makes you happy?

I hope you have the courage to ask these questions. Even if not all of them. Just a handful will do the magic. I would love you to connect with me and tell me about the outcome. You can get in touch with me through social media or on my website WhyAmIStillSingleBook.com

4. Stop Saying You Are Fine

He forgot your birthday. You're fine. He is being rude to your friend. You are fine. He got himself a take-away but didn't ask you if you wanted anything to eat. You are fine. He said something that really hurt you. You are fine. He forgot to tell you he's married. You are still fine.

Everyone is telling you to raise your standards. Raise your standards when you are looking for a job, getting a mortgage, getting a meal, going to the gym. Raise your standards when you are interacting with your friends or having sex. Your standards are supposed to be skyrocket high.

You have seen throughout the book how I encourage you to teach others how you want to be treated. I am a big believer in that. When I look at my past relationships I can see a very clear pattern. The only reason I was hurt was because I did not know any better. I could have walked away anytime. But I was indulging in the pain instead. I did not think of myself as someone that deserved more. I just kept saying I was fine.

Have you ever been in a similar situation? You are being mistreated, but you just can't see it clearly. You are so understanding. You swallow your words. You think it is better to just let it go. You justify. You put yourself second. And you say you are fine.

Next thing you know it becomes your reality. And if you do not have a great support system, if you do not have a tribe that can shake you a little when you are acting like a crazy person, you could be staying there for a very long time.

Maybe you are going through this right now. Being in a situation where you don't see the goddess that you are. The woman that is meant to live the most exciting life filled with love and fun, adventure and inner peace. The woman that is meant to dance with wolves. Not just someone who is fine.

However, sometimes you might be saying that you are fine for other reasons. For a man, it's one of the scariest things in the world. All you are trying to say is that if that person continues along this route you will bring down a series of destructive events upon your head that will rival the world's most destructive historical events. If you are reading this and you have no idea what I am talking about you are not a woman. Or you are just too sophisticated for this BS. Good for you. But a lot of ladies are not like you.

You know those moments when he hasn't picked up your favourite dinner or when he forgets to record your favourite show or ignores you while you are talking to him. When he doesn't appreciate the dinner you cooked or flirts with a waitress. You say you are fine. And then all these ideas come into your head.

You could pick one route and just chill and not be bothered about it. However, there's another route. The drama. The one where you get so carried away that you do not even remember how all this started. You get to the state where you cannot even recognise yourself. But you have gone so deep that your inner psycho is not able to let go. Please stop doing that.

Miscommunication is one of the main reasons you and your partner are not able to understand each other. All you have to do is just say what you want. Then listen to what he says without interrupting him. Listen to what he says not what you think he says.

When he says something, it is not about what he said, but it is all about how he said it. Guess what? Very often you are just projecting. You are a grown-up woman. Talk about what is bothering you, but just keep in mind that very often it is not easy for him to understand what you mean. And you always have a choice. It is up to you how you want to react.

He is not a mind reader. Teach him how you want to be treated. You have so many different sides to yourself. Sometimes you might feel he is your soul mate and other days you might feel that you want to kill him. That's ok. Go for a walk. If he does something that really hurts, you do not say you're fine. Tell him. Don't keep it all bottled up inside of you. It's unhealthy and makes you feel that you are not important.

There is nothing more attractive than the ability to communicate with your partner in a way where you can clearly discuss your concerns and worries. It takes a bad-ass high quality woman to admit when she is being wrong or overreacting. It also takes a very brave one to walk away from someone who hurts her. Stop saying you are fine.

Exercise. *Queen's Tribe.*

Write down names of 10 people that you know.

From your family, personal or business/work related environment.

1. _____

2. _____

3. _____

4. _____

5. _____

6. _____

7. _____

8. _____

9. _____

10. _____

Think of the ways you could improve your relationship with each of them. If you do not feel you would like to do anything to improve your relationship with that person, write down the reason this person is still in your life.

5. He is Not Your Therapist

I am about to share something with you that could give you an answer to something that has been bugging you for a long time. When I learned this, it just made my life so much easier. I wish someone told me about it earlier.

Imagine this situation.

You come back after a long day at work, you must finish a presentation to meet the deadline. Your laptop suddenly decides to die. Your mum calls. She is complaining again about her poor health and her life. She refuses to see a doctor. She starts telling you that you have to hurry up with babies. The clock is ticking. You are not getting any younger. Her best friend's daughter is expecting her second baby and you don't even have a deposit for your mortgage. This is the worst day of your life.

Your very lovely and thoughtful man is next to you listening to your hardships. He is there for you, because he knows that the words of the affirmation and the quality time are your primary love languages. He is there for you. You have taught him well. He knows how important for you is that he listens.

However, at the same time he does not think there's any point in continuing to talk about it. It is time to solve these problems. He comes up with a number of ways to do that. You get annoyed, because you feel that he is not listening. You are tired and exhausted. You don't want to solve anything. You just want him to be here for you and listen. Be there for you a bit longer and listen to you when you go in circles without thinking of any solutions.

He gets confused. There's something you must understand and remember about your communication. When a man is discussing the problem, he is looking for a solution. When you are discussing a problem, very often you just want to discuss it a bit longer. The solution is not what you are after. You just want someone to listen to you. For him this concept is foreign. He is not wired in that way. He is neither your therapist or your girlfriend who doesn't mind going in circles for hours and not getting anywhere.

That is one of the reasons why having your tribe is so important. You want your man to be everything. You want him to be your best friend, your therapist, your shopping buddy, the person you go to the gym with, cook dinners together, watch films and do gardening and the list goes on.

You cannot expect all these things from one person. And if you do, there won't be much space left for all the exciting things you can do together. The intimacy, sex and the playtime. In the past it took the whole village to do things that you are expecting from one man. It simply does not work that way. It could be one of the reasons you are still single. You are expecting to get it all from one person.

Having that special someone is great, but having your tribe is crucial to keep you sane. Go back to *Chapter III* to read about the importance of your network. A powerful tribe of ladies can be a lifesaver when you are going through tough times, when you need someone who can honestly tell you when you are not making the most sensible decisions. A tribe of ladies that keeps you accountable when you want to text that tall, handsome and unavailable. A tribe of ladies that holds your hair when in need.

And you know what? Sometimes it's a good idea to get a therapist or a coach. Sometimes all you need is to just ask yourself better questions, so you can see yourself in a different way. You do not know what you do not know.

I am currently on the waiting list to have some therapy. I had a call last week from one of the places. They asked me some questions. The call lasted for about 45 minutes. They asked me if I felt suicidal, how was my mood, my motivation, my sleeping patterns, my appetite. I told them. They called me a week later saying I would have to get back to them in 6 months when I am totally healed and feeling strong to have the treatment. Interesting.

If you are feeling miserable, down, suicidal or depressed go and seek some help. He is not your therapist. There is something missing in your life and that's the reason you are feeling that way. Could be just a chemical imbalance. It could also be your blueprint or your expectations, your mindset or your childhood trauma. Journal. See if you can dig deeper into yourself. Find someone that can help you, but do not get upset when he does not get you. He is not your therapist. He is not a mind reader.

I would love to share something that I have learned during the *Mindvalley* speaking course I did with Lisa Nichols, a celebrated motivational speaker who has inspired millions through her seminars and her role as a featured teacher in *The Secret*. She is one of the most inspiring ladies that could help you to open up for something you thought was impossible.

When Lisa was going through difficult times she was struggling with depression. She went to see a doctor. She did an exercise that I am about to share with you. When she came back after 30 days to see her doctor he did not recognise her. Lisa was full of light and love, passion and excitement. Just like you were born to be.

Exercise. *Words of Love*

Sit where you won't be disturbed. Think of the moments through your whole life when you felt proud of yourself, what you would like to forgive yourself and what you commit to doing.

Take time to reflect and look for events and achievements in your life that really matter to you. Write them down.

For example,

I am proud of you for leaving that job.
I am proud of you for passing the exams.

I forgive you for letting him hurt you.
I commit to you that I will practice self-love.

Pride

1. I am proud of you for _____
2. I am proud of you for _____
3. I am proud of you for _____
4. I am proud of you for _____
5. I am proud of you for _____
6. I am proud of you for _____
7. I am proud of you for _____

Forgiveness

1. I forgive you for _____
2. I forgive you for _____
3. I forgive you for _____
4. I forgive you for _____
5. I forgive you for _____
6. I forgive you for _____
7. I forgive you for _____

Commitment

1. I commit to you _____
2. I commit to you _____
3. I commit to you _____
4. I commit to you _____
5. I commit to you _____
6. I commit to you _____
7. I commit to you _____

Once you have finished writing all the statements read them again. Then stand in front of the mirror and say it looking at yourself in the mirror. Do it for 30 days.

There is a gift from me to you. A video where I reveal my statements for the moments of pride, forgiveness and commitment. Also, a very interesting statement that one of my clients shared with me. There is a video where I explain in more depth how you should do this exercise and a printout, which you can pin to your wall. Watch the video and get the printout for the *Words of Love* mirror exercise at WhyAmIStillSingleBook.com

6. You Can Have It All

When was the last time you sat down to draw a map of what you would really love in life? When was the last time you sat and thought about what you would like in your relationships, your health, your career, your growth, your body, your environment, your family? How do you know that what you want is coming from you and not from what your family, Disney or Hollywood tells you to do?

No matter how actualised, awake, self-aware you are, you cannot know when what you are chasing or if what you are craving is coming from who you truly are or whether it is just a story you are telling yourself. But there is something you can always do. You can try different things and see what works for you.

You are a beautiful creature, but also a very complicated

one. I don't know about you, but most days I have no idea
what I am doing here. First, I am in a complete denial that I
am an adult. Secondly, I am disappointed in myself that I do
not eat ice cream 24/7, because that's what I was intending
to do when I was 4 years old. I am so confused. Too often I
expect a man that is with me to know my thoughts without
needing to voice them. Isn't that the idea of soul mates that
you were sold on?

I do not believe in soul mates. I do not believe in meeting
someone who will be your perfect other half. It's never going
to be as smooth as when you cut that perfectly ripe avocado.
Disney was wrong. I believe in meeting someone, showing
how messed up you are and having a laugh about it. It's
being with someone who is curious to learn with you and
about you. It's being with someone that feels nice when you
hug him.

Someone that looks at you with eyes full of love, but is
brave enough to say some real stuff when you are arguing
or being out of sorts. Because he trusts you and he feels he
can be vulnerable with you. It's being with someone who
knows you do not like taking out the bin, so he does that for
you. Someone who understands that you get depressed and
you need space, but more than anything you need hugs and
words of affirmation.

Guess what? These magical things do not happen after
the first date. It takes time, work, lots of effort, energy, commitment and patience to get to that degree of understanding. You can never achieve it if you do not know yourself.
You can never achieve it if you think that this person will
be able to fix your life. You can never achieve it if you think
this person is able to be your tribe, your best friend, your

lover, your handy man, your gym and shopping buddy and your book club plus one. It just does not work that way. You need some mystery, you need some excitement to keep things going.

For me, having it all doesn't mean that I will wake up every morning loving life and dancing on rainbows. Having it all means that on the days when I feel like a failure I will still be able to get out of bed and find something to appreciate about my life. Having it all means that I have time to smell the roses and smile when a bird shits on me. Having it all means that I am seeing someone who does not have a perfect body but has the most beautiful heart and is willing to listen when I doubt myself and reminds me it is going to be ok and that I am enough.

Having it all means that I take care of my body, but I let myself have that slice of pie without feeling guilty or not good enough. Having it all means I am doing all I can to live a life where I am growing and progressing, achieving and learning, but I do not feel like a failure when my to do list only involves staying in bed and not killing myself. Then getting up the next day and thanking the universe for removing that dark mist from my eyes.

Having it all means that I have a million things to do and it's making me anxious, but I am going to take an hour for that beautiful walk and some therapy colouring. Having it all means I can explain to my lover how I want to be touched, because I feel no shame and I feel safe. I celebrate my body every single day.

Having it all means I like myself first thing in the morning without having to check my likes on Facebook and Instagram. Having it all means that I acknowledge the fact that I am the most perfect imperfect creature doing my best juggling this thing called life.

Having it all means I am brave enough to open my heart to a complete stranger and enjoy the journey hoping that the little girl inside me will finally find that so desired happily ever after. Even if it means that my Prince Charming could shit on my heart. I can always clean it and spray something floral on it.

Dear Goddess, never stop believing in love. Dance with wolves, be too much. Don't dim your light. Indulge into lots of love.

References

Alain de Botton, *Why You Will Marry the Wrong Person*, The School of Life, 2014,

https://www.youtube.com/watch?v=zuKV2DI9-Jg

Chimamanda Ngozi Adichie, 2012, *We Should All be Feminists*. Vintage Books

Deepak Chopra (1996), *The Seven Spiritual Laws of Success*, Bantam Press.

Gary Chapman (1995), *The Five Love Languages: How to Express Heartfelt Commitment to Your Mate*, Chicago, Moody Publishers.

Gina Hatzis, 2018, *The Too Much Woman*,

https://m.facebook.com/story.php?story_fbid=2044696289118780&id=1399206047001144

Marisa Peer, 2015, Perfect Weight Forever by Marisa Peer, https://www.youtube.com/watch?v=fWXmaLpluOg&t=1047s

Success Magazine, 2017, Mel Robbins: This is Why Women Don't Get Ahead,

https://www.youtube.com/watch?v=2ADB_H3Bi_I

Statistics, 2017, Anorexia & Bulimia Care, http://www.anorexiabulimiacare.org.uk/about/statistics

Do you have a single male friend that could do with some loving?

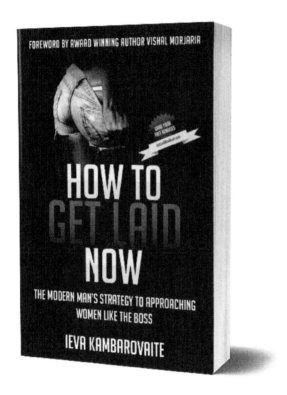

Get him my book HOW TO GET LAID NOW: The Modern Man's Strategy to Approaching Women Like The Boss. Availale on *Amazon*.

GetLaidNowBook.com